"A MESSAGE FROM SIBERIA"

WRITTEN BY: COY REECE HOLLEY

Prov. 10.22; Sgg RH

1

"A MESSAGE FROM SIBERIA"

A BIBLE STUDY CURRICULUM FOR VICTIMS AND OFFENDERS OF DOMESTIC VIOLENCE, SEXUAL ASSAULT, AND OTHER CRIMES AND/OR TRAINING PROGRAM FOR VOLUNTEERS OF SUCH PROGRAMS

TABLE OF CONTENTS

INTRODUCTION—THE FAITH OF INCONVIENENCE

UNIT I--A CALL OUT OF THE PAST INTO HIS MARVELOUS, GLORIOUS LIGHT

UNIT II—SEEING THINGS THROUGH A DIFFERENT PAIR OF GLASSES

UNIT III--THE ROAD BACK HOME TO RECOVERY

UNIT IV--WHERE DOES THE TRAIL (AND MY FUTURE) LEAD TO FROM HERE?

EPILOGUE: A LETTER TO SARAH

INTRODUCTION--THE FAITH OF INCONVIENENCE

One of the problems I have had over the past several years is in trying to force myself to spend time at all even beginning to crack the Word of God. (In fact, I can honestly tell you that I have at least failed personally in this area.) It seems at times that I have immensely succumbed to the temptation of relying on the one and only Christian TV station that I can even receive on my own TV at home and have, for lack of a better term, substituted a program on that channel in the place of a decent Bible study that I could have done on my own. It seems during this stage of my life that I have unfortunately have gotten very lazy and soft in this area--to my shame and regret.

During one of my various attempts to try to rectify this situation in the past, I spent a good bit of time in devotional study of Oswald Chambers' "My Utmost For His Highest" (which I picked up, in all places, from a pile of old books that I saw one time at a church in the city I currently live that hosts a monthly "cowboy church" service). There was a title in this book in one of these studies that might really cause you to stand up and pay attention to what he uses as predominant themes throughout the book: "DO THE THING". It seems to me that Mr. Chambers' brand of Christianity doesn't necessarily allow too much for inaction or inactivity as far as the proclamation of the Gospel goes. And he seems unwilling to pull any punches or cut you any slack in the process. No excuses allowed, no quarter given, and nothing else except unconditional and abject surrender to the Almighty is accepted. Quite an interesting concept that he espouses--but definitely not for those who prefer to remain comfortable.

In thinking about writing what follows, I guess I seem to prefer to operate in a similar vein as Mr. Chambers--but with an additional firm conviction that if I danced around the issues like we will soon be discussing here and if I did not strive to do things right and in a way that would honestly attack some deeper issues in the process, I would be horrifically guilty of doing you a major disservice in the creation and the dissemination of this work.

Some may have visions or dreams, others have a great appetite and interest in God's Word--and while still many more serve as great intercessory prayer warriors. BUT I DO NOT CLAIM BY ANY SHAPE, MANNER, OR FASHION to be ANY of these! Somehow, instead, I seem to feel much more comfortable in the role of DOING more than anything else. Please allow me to introduce the focus of the concept I wish to discuss here by the elaboration of a personal example.

During a period of time when I was regularly going to assist a certain group in the area of prison ministry at a couple of state penal facilities near where I live, I initially depended on rides from one of the men involved with that group in order to even have the privilege of participating (i.e.--if I didn't have a ride, I usually didn't go). But after a while of this, it got to where this method was unreliable on my end-- especially when I personally realized that I was virtually walking the exact same distance on a frequent basis to where I work in the other direction to where I live as where the units close to the city where I live were in relation to where my apartment was.

So finally one night, I decided to do something to test God out and to see how far my faith really was and see how God might probably see my relationship with Him from His perspective. I literally decided to walk to the place where I was going--exactly 3 to 4 miles away. (I figured--hey, even if I was late, at least I'd be getting my exercise and enjoy what I considered my personal weight loss plan at the time--"poverty and walking". Unfortunately, my immense amount of exercise never exactly kept up with my propensity for eating--but, ah well...that's neither here nor there.)

So I experimented with this for a while and took the leap of faith necessary to get to the unit and back--not sticking out my thumb or doing anything that others might interpret as hitchhiking, but just simply relying on Him to virtually take care of my transportation needs to continue my involvement with this group. The results of this experiment were, to say the least, quite fascinating. Not all of the time, but the biggest majority of the time sometime right in the middle of these walks, ten would get you one that somebody would eventually ask if I needed a ride somewhere. Sometimes they were members of the group itself while at other times they were either friends that I knew personally in the past or were total absolute strangers to me. But nevertheless, my God was always faithful and somehow managed to get me there. But the more amazing part of this was that I rarely if ever had to walk back home. This continued for the rest of this period of time that I have opportunity to participate with this group. [Talk about literally walking in faith--I'm a complete walking, talking example of it...]

One night during this particular period of time, as I was going in to the Central Control part of one of the units with this group, I saw (as we would normally do) a couple of men from various Churches of Christ in our city that would usually hold a Bible study at the same time the group I was with would hold our church service. All of us in our group knew them well and as we waited to present our drivers' licenses to the front window for the correctional officers to check their records, one of the men who was the minister of the only Black Church of Christ in our city told me that he saw me as I was walking to the unit as he was passing by in his car. He said to me that he was talking to the other man who was assisting him with their Bible study and telling him, "That young man is dedicated! I think I'll give him a ride..." Unfortunately, by the time he thought this, someone else with a similar notion who was a part of the group that I was with had already beat him to the punch--so he lost his chance. But I was, to say the least, highly flattered by his comment.

But in thinking about this remark in retrospect, I have since developed the opinion that what some people call "dedication" and "going far out of the way" is only to me at best par for the course (at least as far as I and He are both concerned)! What some people would consider work performed above and beyond the call of duty is to me personally simply the commonplace way that I am forced to live and adapt to. And what's worse--I struggle and feel that I must do more than I am doing right now and go past even the mere limitations of what I am able to do personally and that, despite perceptions to the contrary, that I am nowhere close to beginning to do what needs to be done.

But why, you ask, is this so? And why is this conflict taking place within me in the first place? I have struggled in times past to find a quick, shorthand way that's clear and easily understandable to all to say things that I would naturally have a problem in either vocalizing or writing down in a manner that doesn't require immense philosophical or theological debate and that the ordinary man or woman can easily relate to. It is only recently that I now feel that I have found what I feel to be a very apt and suitable term to describe this phenomenon--the thing that I would like to describe as "the faith of inconvenience".

But how exactly should one properly define this so-called "faith of inconvenience"? Allow me to talk about a few other things first before I get to the exact definition that I wish to use and then I believe that the answer that you might be seeking will quickly and easily become apparent. I think that I have an observation on a problem that seems to be rampant here amongst a number of Christians here in our American society. I personally fear that when push comes to shove that there's a majority of Christians have an intense dislike to be inconvienenced in any way, shape, or form (whether it is or is not necessary) and/or a fear of the consequences that might possibly occur (even if it doesn't).

Let's do a wee bit of a comparison/contrast thing to chase this bunny trail to its proper end. For instance, most of the time when my grandparents lived in East Texas, what seemed to be the most unacceptable "inconvienences" involved major catastrophes such as severe illness, death, or things of a much more grave and serious nature. Anything not falling into this categories was considered "shirking"--and those prone to this tendency were usually considered slackards and ne'er-do-wells.

But an unacceptable "inconvienence" in our modern era? How about if your nearby ATM is broke or if someone doesn't move as fast as you like in traffic? Or how about a telemarketer calling during supper (especially on a cell phone)? And bleep forbid that the world should end if you get Extra Crispy instead of Original Recipe at your nearby KFC! Yes, bleep forbid--you need to launch a ICBM missile at a picture of Colonel Sanders for that terrible misdeed against you just because you didn't get exactly what you wanted. (Talk about making mountains out of molehills....)

Again, another comparison/contrast situation...When I was typing up a portion of the history of a church where I formerly worked at as a part-time secretary, I found something interesting about the early days of that church. Some of the records of the meetings of the ladies' auxiliary of that church showed instances where members were actually prevented from attending those meetings due either to heat, weather-related conditions, or inaccessible roads. (Keep in mind that this was in an era BEFORE such things as indoor air-conditioning or automobiles.)

But as for now--people will completely fall apart at Wal-Marts if they either can't find their car keys or have problems remembering where they parked. (Or, just to prove that I'm not immune to these problems and to bring myself down a notch from my so-called "high and mighty throne"-- feeling frustrated when a computer that I might be working on at a certain time doesn't exactly cooperate with me in the exact way that I think it should.)

All in all, I think I've become cognizant of the fact at this stage of my life that we don't exactly see the full and complete picture about what inconvienence truly and fully is. It's not to say that I'm better than anyone else--but I'm grateful in at least one way to Him that there have been various times in my life that I have not been allowed to settle for the routes in my life that have become most convenient. In fact, I can safely say in analysis that a good part of my life thus far to this juncture has been (for lack of a better term) EXTREMELY INCONVIENENT! But I also wonder how totally and radically different that my own life would have been and how dull it could have possibly been had I decided to go with the flow of everyone else and settle for the trails that were the easiest and convenient for me to travel on.

"But you haven't exactly told me what this so-called 'faith of inconvienence' means. Don't beat around the bush, man--tell me what you're saying!" you're probably thinking right now. Okay...here it is--you asked for it. To me, I interpret the meaning of "the faith of inconvienence" as a stepping out of my comfort zone to do things that for me personally are by all outward appearances EXTREMELY inconvienent to do things that I may personally consider ho-hum, but in which to others seems a bit against the grain and extraordinary. Is that a concise enough definition for you or what?

But perhaps if that doesn't convince you, let me add a quick list of a few more personal illustrations that will help remove further doubts from your mind:

(a.) A personal decision I made to become a member of my current church at a time when others considered that church to be a "cult" (in which, I am proud to say, is not regarded as much that these days by a number of prominent members of Christian orthodoxy) at a time of my life when it was truly "inconvienent" and the consequences I suffered as a result of that decision as well as the regrets, mistakes, etc. that have come on me as a result of having to live out what I believed (BUT ALSO, in spite of these difficulties, having the privilege of experiencing firsthand some of the greatest treasures and blessings that have come as a result of it)

(b.) Taking trips for various causes (especially in the area of criminal justice ministry) and on behalf of various people at the sheer and utmost financial risk to myself at times and even causing personal problems with various creditors (my landlord, in particular) as a result

(c.) Giving money, services, etc. that I could have otherwise used personally as seed gifts to others in obedience to Him

But now, why this "faith of inconvienence"? What's so important about it anyway? Well, I can counter with the following: Was it convenient for Avram/Avraham to get out of the land that he lived so that he could go to a place that he didn't know and that he would not have actual claim to during his own lifetime that God highly suggested that Avram should go? Or how about Joseph? Did he in his right mind say, "I want to be sold as a slave by my brothers, mistreated by all, and then, oh, by the way, sometime before my life's through, serve as second-in-command to the most powerful ruler in the world."? I would gather not.

And how about someone named David? Now there's someone whose middle name should have been inconvienence. And time would not permit (to paraphrase another Apostle) to tell about folks like Job or someone like Peter who might walk on water, commit the most stupidest stunts--and yet help lead the Body of Christ through some

8

of its most formative years and die on a cross upside down...or even other folks who didn't mind a little inconvienence on their journey to eternity.

Two quotes stand out in my mind that probably best sum up the essence of this "faith of inconvienence" concept. The first was something out of JFK's first inaugural speech when he talked about putting a man on the moon before the end of the '60s: "We don't do these things because they are easy, but because they are hard." But one of my biggest and favorite quotes is one that used to hang on my refrigerator door at home that MLK, Jr. gave and in which shows me each time I turn around what this "faith of inconvienence" thing's truly all about: "The ultimate measure of a man is not where he stands in moments of comfort and convienence, but where he stands at times of challenge and controversy."

So how would I best appropriately define what follows when I give the "message from Siberia" that I am about to bring? The only way that I think could come close to the mark is this--a call by our God to NOT settle for what is convienent, but rather to live with "the faith of inconvienence". For the spiritual place that I am fixing to describe called "Siberia" DOES NOT naturally lend itself to convienence. In fact, it is going to be one of the harshest routes that you might ever travel.

What is this road like? I can tell you this for a fact--it will require different people to face different challenges that for them are impossible for them to do on their own strength, but in which can only be done with the very grace of the Almighty Father Himself. And for the particular groups that this Bible study curriculum is designed for, surviving in this spiritual Siberia will virtually require you to face up to long-held fears, oppressions, unpleasant memories, etc. that have walked with you side-by-side for many years.

You victims, for instance, may have to eventually come to the realization that what was taken so unjustly from you can never be fully brought back this side of eternity-- and that any wallowing in hatred, loathing, rejection, unforgiveness, and revenge will only hurt you in the end. Those of you that are still incarcerated will eventually have to finally realize for yourself that you might possibly be the ONLY ONE responsible for what you have done and that your actions haven't just hurt you--but others, too, in the process. And the rest of you in the Body of Christ will soon have to realize that there may be at least one more job left undone that may keep us from seeing our Savior's return upon this earth sooner than most of us might like. We have not fully known or realized this work-- and therefore, we must understand that there's still a whole lot more work to do for Him yet. And unnecessary speculations on such subjects as end-time prophecy or other spiritual fads and trends of the day will not get that work done by any means.

But what is even more startling about this landscape is that this Siberia WILL NOT allow you to settle for tolerance and convienence or to simply put up with and cope with certain problems so that you will have a "decent life". The problem with that is that while it may provide you with temporary relief, it does not allow you to shoot for and aim for the higher area of living and excellence that the God that I serve desires, demands, commands, and expects you to live in. AND I ABSOLUTELY REFUSE TO SERVE A GOD OF TOLERANCE AND CONVIENENCE--not when this God says otherwise in His Word through the prophet Isaiah:

"...Who has believed our message and to whom has the arm of the Lord been revealed? He grew up before him like a tender shoot and like a root out of dry ground. He had no beauty or majesty to attract us to him, nothing in his appearance that we should desire him. He was despised and rejected by men, a man of sorrows, and familiar with suffering. Like one from whom men hide their faces, he was despised, and we esteemed him not...

"Surely he took up our infirmities and carried our sorrows, yet we considered him stricken by God, smitten by him, and afflicted. But he was pierced for our transgressions, he was crushed for our iniquities; the punishment that brought us peace was upon him, and by his wounds we are healed." (Isa. 53:1-5, NIV)

THE VERY GOD THAT I SERVE IS NOT A GOD OF TOLERANCE--NO, HE ABJECTLY REFUSES TO BE SUCH!!!!!!!!!!! HE IS NOT THE VERY GOD THAT I SERVE IS NOT A GOD OF TOLERANCE--NO, HE ABJECTLY REFUSES TO BE SUCH!!!!!!!!!!! HE IS NOT A GOD OF TOLERANCE, BUT A GOD OF DELIVERANCE!!!! And I refuse to see that you are tolerant of your pain...that won't cut it for me--and I'm sure, too, that it won't cut it for you, neither. I want to see you SET FREE COMPLETELY from those chains that bind you right now! And you WILL NOT survive in this spiritual Siberia UNLESS AND UNTIL He who is able to TRULY AND COMPLETELY save and deliver you beecomes a part of YOUR life!

Some people will consider me nuts for saying this--and psychologists will try to talk you out of this saying that this type of talk is a bunch of phooey and nonsense! BUT DON'T YOU ACCEPT THAT JUNK FOR ONE MINUTE!! WHY????? Because you know and I know DEEP within each of us that this way--THE one true Way--is the only Way that will ever make sense. And no psychologist, so-called expert, or anyone else will ever convince me otherwise.

I do not honestly claim to know anything myself about what truly happens in any of the situations that we will be discussing in detail in the pages that follow. But I traveled through a spiritual Siberia that might at least relate in some way to what you're dealing with right now. I know because I have personally traveled down this particular road to Siberia and know by experience the exact way this road curves and bends. And this road virtually requires you to have this "faith of inconvenience" in order to survive. This road and this land we are fixing to travel in is definitely NOT for the couch potato or for those who live in flights of unrealistic dreams of living in the lap of opulent luxury.

Only those that are willing to be persistent, diligent, and tenacious in their efforts can expect to go down this road and journey through this harsh spiritual Siberian land. And only those who are willing to do whatever it takes for Him through "the faith of inconvience" can ever expect to excel. And after you've gone through it, you may surprisingly find yourself echoing the reputed words of Russian novelist, dissident, and Nobel laurate Alexander Solzhenitsyn after his own personal release from the actual Siberia in communist Russia--"...Thank you, prison, for having been in my life." As you take this difficult journey, may you in the process also remember to have fun, learn much, and be blessed as you go through your trip! Enjoy the ride!

[SPECIAL CREDITS AND THANKS GO TO THE FOLLOWING FOR THEIR CONTRIBUTIONS TO THIS PROJECT:]

To the staff and management of the Hale County Crisis Center (now known as the Crisis Center of the Plains) (Kay Harris, Executive Director, and Jimmie Kay Moore, former Volunteer Director) for their assistance in providing research materials necessary in relation to the subjects of domestic violence and sexual assault discussed here in this book;

Mr. Mark Ensign, Teaching Elder of the Messianic Jewish Congregations of Adot Adonai (Assembly of the L-rd) in Amarillo and Lubbock, TX for his kind permission in the use of certain portions of his Torah studies as a part of this project;

To my "test driving" team (i.e.--special reviewers during various phases of this project)--Dr. Patricia Herman (West Texas Area Director--Prison Fellowship Ministries), Mr. Don Castleberry (Freedom In Jesus Ministries), et al.

To the various friends, family, and past and present members and pastors of the following churches: Worldwide Church of God congregations throughout the U.S. and the world; St. Mark's Protestant Episcopal Church, Plainview, TX; New Covenant Church, Plainview, TX; and Bro. Frank Hammond of Children's Bread Ministry, Plainview, TX (Their varied contributions and seedings into my life, financial and otherwise, will not be soon forgotten by Him or by me! Baruch HaShem for their faithfulness and obedience to Him!)

This book is officially dedicated to both several women and children (who shall remain nameless for the purposes of this book for obvious reasons) that I know personally and am aware of that have been affected by the spectre of domestic violence and sexual assault as well as prisoners that are also affected by these same issues. May the God of peace that can lead you through this Siberia finally prove Himself able to you to reconcile, heal, and mend the wounds of the past; bring the situation full circle to its full and complete resolution; and lead you safely back home.

See you at the CROSSroads,

(May you be blessed in the name of Y'shua Ha'Meshiach/the Lord Jesus Christ,)

Coy Reece Holley

UNIT I, LESSON I--TRIBAL INITIATION (STARTING OVER IN THE HOUSE THAT MERCY REBUILT)

[Note to Group Leader and Volunteers: Those wishing to study this subject in further detail BEFORE pursuing this lesson are HIGHLY advised to read the book "Healing The Masculine Soul" by Gordon Dalbey published in 1988 by Word Books prior to preparations for this activity. The author of this curriculum especially feels that an IN-DEPTH study of Chapter 3 ("Come Out, Son Of My People") of the Dalbey book beforehand would be especially beneficial to obtain necessary insights into this topic.]

[Main Purpose Of This Group Activity:] To provide those you minister this activity to appropriate affirmation (especially of the masculine kind to young boys and men) and God-honoring unconditional love, respect, and acceptance that these participants may not have otherwise received in the past for various reasons

[Format and Plan of Activity:]

Group Leader and Volunteers:

[PART I:] (1.) It is HIGHLY recommended that this be conducted with a mixed volunteer group of men and women IF AT ALL POSSIBLE. Appropriate adjustments should obviously be made, of course, to how this activity is implemented according to the situation at hand--BUT as a general guideline, this should be conducted with the women in the group playing a CRUCIAL role in this due to the objectives of this lesson.

The aim of this activity is to incite participants to break out of the past and sever all outstanding and inappropriate maternal bonds and allow male participants of this course to start the process of forming healthy relationships with those of their own gender in accordance with Scriptural admonitions. It is advised that the group leader serve as the "spirit" person of this activity that will work to entice participants to join the group. The women in the group, for lack of a better term, will serve as a sort of "villain" that represents the natural maternal instinct to continue the mother/child relationship that a mother typically enjoys with her son. The other men, on the other hand, will stand behind the "spirit" person as a way to encourage the new participant to, figuratively, join the corporate fellowship of other men.

(2.) Your general script for this activity is extremely simple: Depending on the situation, the group leader will then BEFORE the activity starts arrange for suitable positions and procedures of both volunteer groups to operate within the appropriate parameters of the activity.

[SPECIAL NOTE: IF you are doing this within the confines of a prison setting or a place requiring higher security than usual, it is HIGHLY essential that this be cleared with appropriate officials of the facility and that any staff working in the facility be aware of what will be taking place during this activity so that appropriate security measures can be put in place and adhered to. ALSO--it is MANDATORY that if this activity is allowed to be pursued within such facilities that ALL volunteers adhere to ALL policies and requirements of such institutions!!! IF such accommodations CAN NOT BE ABSOLUTELY MADE FOR ANY REASON to insure the successful implementation of this activity, then it is MANDATORY that this lesson be COMPLETELY skipped and scrapped and that an alternate message, lesson, etc. be available for use as a back-up plan.]

The women of the group will serve, in essence, as a protective shield and barrier between participants representing the maternal bonds of the mother and the group leader and other members of the volunteer group. The women should DEFINITELY feel free to play a role in this activity that aims to "hinder" participants from participating. Appropriate improvisations and liberties should be taken by the women to act as if they were the participant's mother and are insistent on preventing the other group from taking the participant with them.

The men's group, meantime, should aim to "call" the participant out--NOT by force, but by respectful encouragement and enticement of the participant to join the group. The group leader/"spirit" person will play a pivotal role in setting the tone here. The "spirit" person should consider the utilization of some sort of TASTEFUL disguise as a way of further enhancing the effect and impact of this activity upon the participants.

Upon the beginning of initial approaches of participants, the men's group should join together in the singing of appropriate hymns behind the "spirit" person. If a male authority figure of the particular institution, etc. is present, he should also be encouraged and asked if possible and otherwise feasible to take part as a part of the men's group as a way to both insure the legitimacy and support of such activity AND to play a direct part in encouraging the participant to "join" the group of men.

(3.) As men's group makes their initial approach to the participant/initiate--The men's group should start singing appropriate hymns (music used by such groups by Promise Keepers, etc. would be recommended and highly appropriate here) as they make their approach.

The women's group and the "spirit" person should continue this little conflict for about two or three tries or so until the women's group finally gives in and steps aside. The participant should then be truly baffled at this little spectacle and confused as to what to do. The men's group and "spirit" person should then "step up the pressure" on the participant to go over and join the growing men's group.

Once participant(s) make their firm decisions on what to do and join the larger group of men, backslaps, "Hallulujah!"s, bearhugs, etc. should follow and encompass the new participant/initiate as they become a part of the larger group. THIS IS THE OCCASION FOR THE MEN'S GROUP TO MAKE SOME NOISE, REJOICE, AND HOOP AND HOLLAR IT UP! The women's group, in contrast, will represent the agony of the women and cry or make some sort of appropriate display and grief over the participant's "...defection to the OTHER side." THIS IS MEANT TO WORK IN A STATE OF ORGANIZED CHAOS--TREAT IT APPROPRIATELY!! Once new participant assimilates into the larger men's group, the process repeats again and again until all participants are present and accounted for and the overall group that will be in attendance has been completely assembled.

[Note: As alluded to earlier, DO NOT be afraid if necessary to make appropriate adaptations to this little game/activity as necessary according to the environment in which you are operating in.]

[PART II:] [FOR USE ONLY IF THIS IS USED AS AN INTRODUCTION TO A SEMINAR OR EXTENDED BIBLE STUDY COURSE]
Once Part I of this "initiation ceremony" has been completed, both volunteer groups will then merge back into one cohesive group to help in the further process of ministry. The Group Leader will then take off his disguise and explain to the participants the nature of the activity that they have just went through and appropriately explain the purposes for why it took place. If this lesson is to serve as the introduction for a weekend seminar OR an extended course dealing with the areas of domestic violence, sexual assault, etc., then this juncture would be the appropriate place to go into detail with the participants about the objectives and aims of the upcoming seminar/course. [If this is to be used ONLY within the context of an introduction of a sermon, the Group Leader should skip IMMEDIATELY to the next section for further instructions.]

The Group Leader should then discuss IN DETAIL the following objectives of the seminar/course (along with any others that are necessary and appropriate):

(1.) To serve as a call for seminar/course participants [(Ex.) If men in prison--to break out of their unhealthy "maternal bonds"] to "come out" of their past and invite them to partake of God's love, grace, and mercy

(2.) To show and demonstrate the TRUE love of the Father and His desire to bless us and show us how much He loves us

(3.) To call participants out of the past that has hindered them (Philippians 3:12-14), stop the excuses ONCE and for ALL, learn to take responsibility for their own actions, and come take part in His "wondrous, glorious light" that he has given us

(4.) To help participants learn to see various issues in the areas of domestic violence and sexual assault in a totally different light

[PART III.] If a sermon is to be used here, this is the place to insert it. OTHERWISE, go to:

[PART IV.] Invitation as needed and possible [Personal recommendation-"The House That Mercy Built", Point of Grace; BUT the choice of music for the invitation can be left to the discretion of the Group Leader and/or other designated individuals!]

[PART V.] Appropriate closing prayers over participants AND the invocation of "The Father's Blessing" by Bro. Frank Hammond of Children's Bread Ministry

[NOTE TO GROUP LEADER: THIS IS THE MOST CRUCIAL PIVOTAL POINT OF THE SERVICE OF WHERE EVERYTHING ELSE SHOULD EVENTUALLY LEAD UP TO! PLEASE TREAT IT APPROPRIATELY AND ALLOW GOD'S SPIRIT TO HELP YOU SET THE APPROPRIATE TONE NECESSARY FOR THIS SECTION OF THE SERVICE!]

BEFORE the Group Leader or whoever he/she designates for the duty prays "The Father's Blessing" over the participants, the Group Leader should say this to the participants:

Group Leader: Let me ask you--how many of you come from broken homes? How many of you have never been blessed by your father or some other sort of male father figure? [Ask for a show of hands.] Do you know that there is POWER in the blessing of a child by his father? People throughout the centuries--EVEN Biblical figures have literally begged, borrowed, stolen, lied, or even killed just to get it. Frank Hammond says this about this thing called "The Father's Blessing":

"Have you received a father's blessing? Did your father ever bless you with loving, prophetic words of acceptance, approval, and divine benediction? If not, then you have missed a very important and valuable gift. Everyone needs a father's blessing. It has power to heal the wounded spirit and to engender Father God's blessing.

"The pattern for the father's blessing is found in God the Father's blessings upon His children. For example: (1.) God blessed His first children, Adam and Eve. 'God blessed them, and God said unto them Be fruitful, and multiply and replenish the earth, and subdue it: and have dominion.' (Gen. 2:28) (2.) 'And God blessed Noah and his sons, and said unto them, Be fruitful, and multiply, and replenish the earth..." (Gen. 9:1) (3.) 'And God said to Abram...I will make of thee a great nation, and I will bless thee and make thy name great, and thous shalt be a blessing.' (Gen. 12:2)

"Furthermore, the Old Testament patriarchs blessed their children. (1.) Isaac blessed his son, Jacob. (Gen. 27:28-29) His father's blessing was of such importance that Jacob lied, deceived, and risked his life in order to obtain it. (2.) Jacob blessed his twelve sons (Gen. 49:). "All these are the twelve tribes of Israel: and this is that their father spake unto them, and blessed them: EVERY ONE ACCORDING TO HIS BLESSING HE BLESSED THEM' (v. 28). In other words, the blessings were personal and prophetic. (3.) Jacob blessed his grandchildren, Ephraim and Manasseh. (Gen. 48:16). (4.) Also, after David had returned the Ark of the Covenant to Zion, "David returned to bless his household." (II Sam. 6:20)

"One of the most precious and valuable things that a father can give his children is "the father's blessing". It is clearly a stabilizing factor in a child's life. Without this blessing there will always be a sense of something missing, a void is created that nothing else can fill. Without the father's blessing there remains a curse.

"Everywhere I go now, I instruct fathers on the importance of blessing their children--even when those children are grown men and women. A father needs to lay hands on the heads of his children and verbalize his love and pronounce his blessings and the blessings of God over them. The father's blessing literally opens the door to receiving Father God's blessings. This is seen in God's commission to Aaron and the priesthood to bless the children of Israel, 'And they [Aaron and the sons of Levi] shall put my name upon the children of Israel; AND I WILL BLESS THEM'. (Num. 6:22-27)...

Do you yearn for the father's blessings that you've never had? It is not too late! Although I may never have the opportunity to lay my hands on your head and bless you in person, you will surely be blessed as you receive the following father's blessing that is prayerfully offered for you. This blessing is for YOU!! Claim it for yourself.

There's something else I feel that I must say before I pray this blessing over you. Let me ask you--do you know why most Jewish families throughout the world have EXTREMELY low instances of crime and also in spite of being one of the smallest people groups in the world have actually won the most Nobel Prizes in various fields of endeavor? It might be because of something that these families do everytime they worship or do something in some way that they feel honors God (especially on the Sabbath). The father in these Jewish families ACTUALLY prays over his wife and his children certain prayers that at the same time express his expectations for them and his high hopes that he is confident that they will live up to them. And the impact that this has carries on throughout all of their generations to come.

I want to do something different that will help bring this even closer to home to you-- I want to pray the following prayer so that it will carry the POWER YOU NEED to get you through when times are tough. When that temptation comes to steal something or to do something that you know isn't right, I WANT YOU TO BURN THIS PRAYER INTO YOUR MIND SO THAT YOU'LL NEVER FORGET IT!! Please bow your heads and listen closely to the words--for my God will use these words in such a way that they will DEFINITELY change your life forever!

A FATHER'S BLESSING

My child, you are a gift from God. I thank God for allowing me to be your father. I want you to know that you are very precious. I love you! You have given me much joy, and I am so very proud of you. I bless you with healing from all the wounds that I and others have caused. I bless you with overflowing peace, the peace that only Jesus, the Prince of Peace, provides. I bless you with fruitfulness in life--good fruit, much fruit and fruit that remains.

You are the head and not the tail, above and not beneath. I bless you with prosperity, for you will prosper and be in health even as your soul prospers. I bless you with spiritual influence, for you are the light of the world and the salt of the earth. I bless you with success, for your meditation upon the Word of God will make you like a tree planted by rivers of water, and your way will be prosperous, and you will have good success.

I bless you with a greater depth of spiritual understanding and a closer walk with your Lord. You will not stumble or falter, for the Word is a lamp unto your feet and a light unto your path. I bless you with pure and edifying relationships in life. I bless you with abounding love, enabling you to minister God's comforting grace to other. You are blessed, my child! You are blessed with all spiritual blessings in Christ Jesus. AMEN!!

[Note to Group Leader: After the above prayer has been prayed, as the Spirit moves you, you are free to add a closing prayer of your own choosing as necessary--after which the service/lesson can then end.]

UNIT I, LESSON II: PRISONS OF OUR OWN MAKING WHERE THE TRUE DISTORTION LIES

I once had a friend in my church who I met one time at a church activity in Fort Worth who I had the privilege of corresponding with via snail mail. We would play chess by mail (which, FYI, we never quite got to finish) and send certain information about ourselves back and forth. I would usually write longer letters while he would tend to respond back by postcards.

In the course of our letters, I had mentioned to him my increasing interest in the area of prison ministry. He wrote back to me one time something that was very short and sweet--but has proved to be a very profound thought that has never escaped me since: "We all live in prisons of our own making--and we don't even know that we have the Key (this presumably meaning our Savior Jesus Christ)."

That made me think VERY deeply about how we sometimes think about how we get into the trails, sufferings, and problems that we all face. The question we might want to think about, though, is--HOW DID WE GET THERE IN THE FIRST PLACE??? Here might be some possible reasons that we might usually offer as excuses:

(1.) My childhood upbringing
(2.) The social environment I was raised in (Poverty? Wealth?)
(3.) Peer pressure
(4.) Rejection from various sources (feeling unloved, etc.)

Some people--RIGHTLY OR WRONGLY--assume that they have valid and proper reasons for their behavior. But, unfortunately, those exact same reasons can be turned into crutches or excuses that keep someone from making necessary changes that can dramatically alter their life and allow themselves to be pleasing to God and to be transformed by His saving grace and power. Let me ask this--could a possible reason for your impending destruction that you're facing now be partly because you are right now in a "prison of your own making"? Let me add another possible reason to the above list:

********(5.) In Act II of the Andrew Lloyd Webber musical "Phantom of the Opera", Christine Dyae sorrowfully sings this line to the Phantom, "This horrid face holds no horror for me now.../It's in your soul where the true distortion lies."

We can't always spend our time blaming our past actions on the faults of other people or society around us because it simply wastes energy, tires us out, wastes what little precious time that we have available to us, and spins our wheels in a way that gets us nowhere! But what does GOD'S WORD possibly have to say about this? The Apostle Paul shoots back with what He said in verses 10-18 of the third chapter of Romans. (Read Rom. 3:10-18 NOW!) How do we truly see ourselves in our own eyes? But also more importantly, how does GOD want us to see ourselves in our eyes? (Read James 1:22-25.)

All of this makes us realize that we simply CANNOT DO THESE THINGS ALONE!! One thing above all else that you must realize about the issues of domestic violence and sexual assault is that one who does these things isn't simply causing physical harm or problems for someone else. On the contrary, these are problems that kill the spirit. They kill dreams and hopes and take away ANY sense of security that victim once had of himself or herself.

There is absolutely NO justification in Scripture that says that a man should EVER beat a woman to a pulp for any reason he desires or give in to an urge to rape and force sex on a woman that does not want it (ESPECIALLY from someone she does not know)--ABSOLUTELY NONE!!!!!! Just because a woman dresses in a manner that gets your desires going at a certain moment in time DOES NOT mean that you have the right to touch her in ANY WAY!!! She does NOT "...deserve to be raped" or "...need to be put in her place" through beating her black and blue and abusing her.

The bottom line is that domestic violence and sexual assault is NOT an issue of sex or the improper fulfillment of uncontrollable lusts, passions, and desires. It's instead an issue of POWER AND CONTROL!! In committing these acts, you are in essence telling a woman, "I cannot control myself. I am insecure and don't know how I feel. There's something I didn't get from someone else--so I'm retaliating against them by taking it out on YOU because I can CONTROL YOU and manipulate you to get what I want--OR I will kill you or make your life a living H---!!" Now when the Apostle Paul told the Galatians that one of the fruits of the Spirit was SELF-CONTROL--ISN'T THAT A STUPID, STUPID WAY TO BEHAVE YOURSELF OR WHAT?????????? Our Adversary has really done a number on us by getting us to act this way. It's like the classic example of drinking poison yourself and expecting someone else to hurt or even possibly die from it.

BUT WHAT DOES GOD SAY THAT YOU CAN START DOING NOW TO CHANGE YOUR SITUATION FOR THE BETTER?

(1.) Admit to God and continually seek Him about this that you have a problem in these areas and ask him to forgive you of these sins against Him and others you directly and/or indirectly have hurt and that He would help you in overcoming these problems. (Read 1 John 1:9!)

(2.) Make a fixed resolution to NOT do these things AGAIN--AND MEAN IT...and to avoid even the mere thought of doing so. Put as many fences as you can that would separate you from those evil inclinations that have plagued you in the past and assist you in getting you away from even the slightest appearance of it. (Read Isa. 50:7; Job 31:1-12!)

(3.) Take AGGRESSIVE steps to put that resolution in place and make the changes you need to make into ACTION!!! Get rid of those distorted thoughts and REPLACE them with these things that are of God. (Read 1 Cor. 13:11-13; Gal. 5:16-26; Phil. 2:1-11 AND 4:8 & 9.]

Folks, find out where the true distortion lies--and who, how, and what needs to change--and then DO IT!!! And I believe that in doing this that YOU in turn will be blessed with a new nature from your God and with a new person that you have never seen before.

[DISCUSSION QUESTIONS AND HOMEWORK:]
(1.) What caused you to be in the situation that you're in right now? Who are you blaming for it?

(2.) Where has all of this led you? What was the result of it all?
********(3.) WHAT ARE YOU GOING TO DO NOW TO CHANGE IT????
Draw up a WRITTEN plan that describes TANGIBLE steps you can take to change the behaviors that led you to beat some woman you once loved or act out sexually in a wrong way. Then, START the process of putting this plan in action.

[Prayer:] Creator Father, Lord God Almighty, and Lord Jesus/Y'shua: Thank you today for teaching me about certain things in my life that led me to make the mistakes that got me to the place where I am right now. Help me now to make a plan that I can put into action RIGHT NOW that will help me to steer clear of those things that caused me to pursue bad behaviors and to instead do those things that would be pleasing to You. Give me YOUR wisdom and ability to do this so that I can truly be more than a conqueror in You. I thank you for this in Your Son's Name--AMEN!!

UNIT I, LESSON III--"IFCOMES"

In the previous chapter, we dealt with discovering "where the true distortion lies" and finding out some reasons that folks might turn into excuses to justify bad behavior. For this lesson, I want to take some time to focus in on something else that might be a deeper cause of problems that might lead to acting out in violent and/or inappropriate ways--the unwillingness to take responsibility for actions that we take that might inflict harm of ANY kind toward others.

To start with, allow me to share a personal story. I had just about finished about all of my studies at Eastern New Mexico University EXCEPT for two things that I had to do to complete my degree in Music Business: one, a REQUIRED internship somewhere within my desired career field; and two, retaking a Corporate Finance course that I had failed two previous times at the main campus. Little did I know how much trouble that all of this would cause me later on down the road.

Through various circumstances, I wound up in Albuquerque, NM having MAJOR problems trying to support myself financially and just couldn't seem to get things right. I was a little bit too proud to take ANY job that didn't fit into my little plans that I had made. I also took on medical expenses on a cataract surgery on my right eye immediately followed just two months later by another one for a detached retina in that very same eye that there was NO way I could even think of paying off anywhere in my lifetime on my own at that particular time in my life because I had no health insurance.

But what was even more of a mistake than anything else I had done was to buy a car from someone at work whose title had not changed hands in at least four previous owners at the time I got it (...who knows if it was possibly stolen...) with money I couldn't realistically part with because I should have used it to take care of my rent (which I was SEVERELY behind in at the time). (By the way, I also had no insurance on the car as well.) Guess how much that car cost me? The grand total of $375 got me the following:
(1.) A car that was a VERY expensive ride for me because I only got to drive it twice since I couldn't afford the insurance, license plate, or other stuff that I needed in order to use it legally
(2.) Two traffic tickets that eventually required me to spend about three days of community service to pay it off by picking up trash on the side of the road in an Albuquerque suburb

But it also caused a couple of other people in my church some problems, too, because:

(3.) It wrecked a relationship of trust between one of my friends in my church and an auto mechanic he dealt with (which, incidentally, he took that car I bought on a mechanic's lien because I couldn't afford to pay for the repairs on it)

Other events escalated to a time that I remember well and which served to be one of the major turning points of my life. One day, when I was in my apartment, the associate pastor and one of my fellow members of the men's club of my church knocked on my door and asked to talk to me for a little bit. What followed next was the equivalent of a confrontation that someone in Alcoholics Anonymous might give to a drunk.

They sat down and expressed their concern for the financial condition that I was in. I tried to deny it and put a good spin on it, but they saw right through my disguise. It was to them the last straw when I pulled that stunt with the auto mechanic. Then, the friend said something that had haunted me since throughout the years--"'Ifcomes' don't work in Satan's world." What this man meant by an "ifcome" is "'...if it comes, I will pay.'" To make the long story short, the whole episode ended in disaster and eventually forced me to move back home. But nevertheless for me, it proved to be a lesson well-learned later on.

Let me ask you this--how many people do you know of personally have been willing to take the blame and responsibility for something they did WITHOUT at the same time trying to justify what they did or shift the blame on someone else? How many do you know that would be honest enough to say, "I'm sorry--it's no one else's fault but mine. There's no one else to blame for it but me. I take full responsibility for it." Rare is the camper that is sincerely and honestly willing to do just that.

But the even more penetrating questions I want to ask of you are these: Are YOU willing to take responsibility for your actions? Are YOU willing to say "I've messed up here." and NOT try to explain it away or blame somebody else for it? And are YOU willing to do everything possible to make amends for past you have done, mend relationships you have broken in the past, and strive NOT to do those very same things again?

Let's even ask a much more deeper and convicting question of ourselves: Is part of the reason why you are in the particular problem that you're in now partly due to an unwillingness to take responsibility for your actions? I don't know--I can't dare personally tell you whether it is or not. That is simply something that you might need to talk to God about yourself to see if that is an issue that you must deal with. Maybe, though, I can be of a little help to you in this process by allowing you to have an opportunity to go a bit in-depth in an area of Scripture that most people might normally miss, but that might at the same time hit you closer to home here. (Read Ex. 21:12-36.)

I think that a Torah study (in otherwords, for those of you that are not familiar with Judaism--a DETAILED and thorough study of a weekly portion of the first five books of the Old Testament) that I one time received via e-mail from Mark Ensign might lend a little bit of unique perspective to this discussion. Mr. Ensign not only is the Teaching Elder of a Messianic Jewish congregation, but also happens to be a practicing attorney and CPA as well--so I think that he would be VERY well-qualified in many ways to speak here about our subject today:

"...Murder, Injuries, and Damage:

"As an attorney I am especially interested in certain aspects of this parsha [Torah portion] as they involve the instructions of our Father regarding our relationship with our fellow men and their property. From these instructions have come many of the criminal and civil laws we have in our justice system today, not only in the United States but also in the civilized world.

"YHVH has set down some general principles which then have exceptions which typically modify and lessen the punishment. A good example is that of a man who strikes another man so that he dies which, YHVH instructs, shall result in the death of the perpetrator. He even specifies that if this person intentionally murdered this fellow that the authorities could take this perpetrator away from the altar of HaShem to which he was clinging as a sanctuary and execute him.

"However, HaShem provides that if this was an unintentional death, he would provide a place to which the person who caused the death could flee which we know as the Cities of Refuge established by HaShem later in the Torah. Thus we see how YHVH is both a G-d of justice and of mercy authorizing swift and final punishment for those guilty of murder while providing a means of mercy to those who unintentionally killed another person.

"Furthermore, YHVH provides that if a person kidnaps a man and sells him as a slave, the kidnapper shall be put to death for selling that person into slavery for doing so is like condemning him to a death sentence. Demonstrating the inequality between a master and his slave as well as the importance of human life, even that of a slave.

YHVH provided that if a master killed his slave, he too would die. So important is YHVH's first instruction with promise, "Honor your father and mother," that he provides that one who either strikes or curses his father or mother shall be put to death. Just imagine how few disciplinary problems and juvenile delinquents we would have today if these rules had been enforced through the ages.

"...YHVH, in his infinite wisdom, understood that men would quarrel and fight resulting in injury but not necessarily death. So he provides that if the injured party recovered, then the perpetrator would not be guilty but would only have to pay for the lost time and the medical expenses of the injured party. This would also be true if men fought and collided with a pregnant woman who miscarried but did not die. The father of the unborn child could collect damages against the perpetrator but the perpetrator would not die as this was an accidental death of the fetus.

"...If the mother had died, then the perpetrator would also have died, "a life for a life". Note in verse 24 the famous phrases, "an eye for an eye, a tooth for a tooth," etc. If the woman who miscarried also suffered injuries, then her assailant had to pay damages to her. The sages report in the Talmud and Machilta [secondary Jewish literature and reference sources] that these phrases indicated that the assailant must pay the monetary value for the injury, such as the value of an eye in restoration for the eye that he had blinded. As the Chumash [the Artscroll translation of the first five books of the Old Testament] reports, "Never was there a Jewish court that ever blinded or otherwise inflicted a physical injury in revenge or retribution; the only corporal punishment ever imposed are the death penalty and lashes, where provided by the Torah...

"...Lastly, as a general rule, if a person damaged the property of another person, the responsible party was expected to pay damages measured in the value of the property lost. The assessments of YHVH in such circumstances appear reasonable to the civilized mind. But when a person intentionally deprived another person of his property, then there was a greater assessment such as that provided in verse 37--five times the number of cattle stolen and four times the number of sheep stolen..."

Now aren't you glad that you're serving time here in the good ol' US of A instead of Ancient Israel, eh? It seems that our God might have much higher expectations of how you should live than you might even have of yourself. But that's NOT because He's constantly "out to get you" or zap you every time you make a mistake. To the contrary, he has these expectations of you for a GOOD and FULFILLING purpose.

But why does God have these high expectations of you? Because of what Peter himself said when we read 1 Peter 2:4-12! God refuses to allow you to dodge responsibility for your actions. You have to face the music sometime--WHY NOT LET IT BE NOW????

[OTHER VERSES TO READ:]
   2 Thess. 3:6-14
   1 Tim. 4:1-16
   1 Chron. 21: [King David]
   2 Sam. chapters 11 & 12

[DISCUSSION QUESTIONS AND HOMEWORK:]

(1.) How did you do on last week's homework assignment? Did you make a plan like you were asked to do? What is it? Have you seen any changes in your life so far as a result of putting that plan into action? What things do you still need to do yet in order to make that plan a continual reality?

(2.) What things (if any) have you dodged responsibility for? Have you shifted blame on something to someone else--OR have YOU been willing to take the fall for what you have done?

(3.) What reasons or excuses have you used to dodge or avoid taking responsibility and/or facing the consequences of your actions?

(4.) How does this failure to take responsibility for certain actions relate to any problems that you might have in the areas of domestic violence and/or sexual assault? What consequences does this bring?

(5.) What can YOU do personally to develop a sense of responsibility in yourself? How can YOU show others that you are a responsible person?

(6.) [HOMEWORK:] During the next week, if and when you do something stupid or wrong, STOP THE BLAME GAME!! Practice taking sole responsibility for your actions and start steps that will demonstrate to others that you are a responsible, trustworthy, and reliable person. [Also--continue working on your assignment from last week as well!]

[PRAYER:] Creator Father, God Almighty, and Lord Jesus/Y'shua: Thank you for helping me to realize the importance of responsibility in the way YOU see it and how it can change my life as well as others that I see every day. Work with me, change my life, and mold it in such a way to where I can be the most honest and responsible person that You have made me to be and let that be easily seen by others. In His name I pray--AMEN!!

UNIT II, LESSON 1--All That Really Glitters Is Not Gold

The following that I am about to say in this lesson is very hard for me to talk about because it deals with subject areas that I have deep personal experience with and which hits me right at home. In fact (sad to say), it might show you better than anything else and help you better decide your opinion of what you personally think of my own personal character and integrity and the stuff I have written about. If you haven't decided yet for yourself whether I am just a "holier-that-thou" hypocrite who thinks that he knows EVERYTHING that is best for you or not OR if I am simply someone who is willing to be so transparent enough to reveal even his most deepest and darkest secrets in a manner that might more fully demonstrate whether or not the fruits of His Spirit are truly at work inside of me, maybe what follows will finally set the record straight once and for all.

In revealing what I am about to say here, I personally face a much harder struggle in which part of the process of writing this in essence involves "crucifying my own flesh". Why do I struggle with this? It is exactly because there are naturally some secrets I want to keep far away from the view of others that in revealing them I would fear it would dramatically cause the perceptions of other people around me about how they view me as a servant of my Lord and would put a kink in the pleasant, non-controversial face I might want to put out for others to see instead of this hideous monster that I not even in my own insane mind would ever wish to see the light of day. It is a monster that even showed his face to me just today as I wrote this and in which--to my shame and embarrassment--gave in to once again.

I ask you--have you maybe faced that same monster, too? Oh, that face is so beautiful, so attractive at first, and so utterly hard to resist on the surface--but, oh, so, so hard to run from and escape from and so hard to look upon after the initial pleasure of the moment has subsided. OH, HOW I COULD WISH SO DESPERATELY THAT I COULD KEEP THESE SECRETS TO MYSELF--but I can't...He just keeps compelling me to reveal them instead--AND HOW I DARE BE DISOBEDIENT TO WHAT MY MASTER AND SAVIOR AND LORD HAS ASKED ME TO DO?? But it is SO, SO HARD to crucify my flesh in this way--but I have no other choice in doing so. Not if the ultimate purpose in writing this is being of service to my Savior will help set you free...

I come in to this with the words of the Rav Shaul (the Apostle Paul) when he said to the Romans, "...We know the law is spiritual, but I am unspiritual, sold as a slave to sin. I do not understand what I do. For what I want to do I do not do, but what I hate I do. And if I do what I do not want to do, I agree that the law is good. As it is, it is no longer I myself who do it, but it is sin living in me. I know that nothing good lives in me, that is in my sinful nature. For I have the desire to do what is good, but I cannot carry it out. For what I do is not the good I want to do; no, the evil I do not want to do--this I keep doing. Now if I do what I do not want to do, it is no longer I who do it, but it is sin living in me that does it...." (Rom. 7:14-20)

That's where even more I seem to delight in jubilant passages like that Paul wrote to the Corinthians about his weakness: "To keep me from becoming conceited because of these surpassingly great revelations, there was given me a thorn in my flesh, a messenger of Satan, to torment me. Three times I pleaded with the Lord to take it away from me. But he said to me, 'My grace is sufficient for you, for my power is made perfect in weakness.' Therefore I will boast all the more gladly about my weaknesses, so that Christ's power may rest on me. That is why, for Christ's sake, I delight in weaknesses, in insults, in hardships, in persecutions, in difficulties. For when I am weak, then I am strong." (2 Cor. 12:7-10)

That's when I try to remember in my stubborn, stupid little head that maybe if even Paul had to face a few bumps in the road and could yet still talk about them with boldness and with true joy in his heart, maybe this ol' West Texas boy could walk a mile in this Jewish rabbi's footsteps and do the exact same thing, too. Maybe I don't have to be perfect after all in order to talk about this stuff--maybe I don't have to be a straw-man image of "Mr. Goody Two-Shoes" to talk about this stuff. I just have to be me and let the Holy Spirit use me as He wills--NOT as I will. My natural tendency on this is to clam up, shut up, and be silent. But HE wants me in contrast to scream aloud to the world about this--so reluctantly I plod on for the purpose of His Gospel on this.

Oh, by the way--the subjects, you ask? To paraphrase the Narrator of Wynton Marsalis's "A Fiddler's Tale"--THE SUBJECT IS WAR!! More specifically, this is a personal declaration of war against some stuff that has wrecked havoc in many lives--even mine. WHY? Because I am a personal casualty of that war--and it has caused a small bit of destruction in my own life. And, worse than that, I fear that it may have scarred yours, too. It's not violence in Israel or Northern Ireland--NO! We're dealing with the subjects of pornography, lust, masturbation, and sexual obsessions and addictions and the ultimate pain and heartache it truly causes in our lives today. And in this war, there are ultimately no winners EXCEPT those who struggle through Christ and find freedom through Him alone. And even then, it will be a hard row to hoe to get out of it and stay out.

I will write about this subject coming from many different directions. The first one I will need to go and take you towards is the hardest one for me to travel back towards--for it forces me to confront past issues and memories of my own past stupidity and makes me reveal things about myself to you that in the natural I would prefer remain buried. There will be other lessons in which I will readily admit that I have absolutely NO knowledge or experience in. But this one IS NOT one of those. In fact, I have seen this hideous monster MANY times and can even tell you the wrinkles on its face right down to the last detail.

[NOTE FOR PARENTS AND OTHER READERS THAT ARE SENSITIVE IN THEIR READING TASTES: Please keep in that the following materials that I am about to discuss here may get a little bit more graphic and explicit (sexual and otherwise) than you may be accustomed to. THEREFORE, those with young children and other sensitive readers ARE HIGHLY ENCOURAGED AND ADVISED to skip the remaining portions of this lesson and move on to the next lesson.]

My problems with masturbation started even when I was a kid in junior high and high school--naturally occurring as thoughts I had towards a certain young lady that I had an intense crush on for several years, but was not able to have any sort of dating relationship with for various reasons (being the son of a single mother being one of them). The lustful thoughts and sexual fantasies that I would entertain in the performance of such an act might vent the frustrations of not being able to fulfill my selfish personal teenage sexual longings. But they did not end even after any hopes of my unrequited love (or at least in the way I thought of as love at the time) towards that young lady faded. In fact, time would intensify those inappropriate cravings more and more. (Have I shattered your illusions and image of your "perfect prison ministry volunteer" yet? I hope I have by now. If not, read more--I'll be busting more of this with a sledgehammer by the time I'm through here.)

At a time when I was struggling a lot with my own personal religious identity, I began also to experiment in inappropriate ways when I went to junior college as well. You have to understand something before I go into detail with this--all during the time during my school years before college, close friendships (ESPECIALLY with those of the opposite sex) were at times few and far between. I usually felt like Norm on the TV sitcom "Cheers" that everyone knew--but I was at the same time lonely, too. I didn't even get to drive a car for ANYTHING until I was a senior in high school--and by then, all of the girls that I might have had an interest in dating were already involved in some seriousrelationships. I couldn't get a date with a girl even if I tried. My situation was so bad datingwise that I even went to BOTH my Junior and

Senior Proms alone. I was able to dance with other girls--but none of them were my dates.

When I got into junior college, though, the scene was a little bit different. Still no real dates of any kind there--BUT I got introduced my first year there to pornography in its purest form. I do NOT want get your imagination going too much further in this--for I do not feel that it is appropriate for me to do so and that revealing such information about the contents of the materials I consumed in the past is important for accomplishing the purposes I wish to achieve here in this brief discussion. In this part of the journey to one of my parts of this abyss, I to my shame consumed certain sexually explicit pornographic magazines containing images of women that were degrading and unfit for perusing and viewing. I also had opportunity to view certain pornographic films with risque materials that were not honoring or pleasing to the God I serve now.

But that didn't compare to what happened one summer when I went to summer school and stayed at what were during the rest of the academic year apartments for the young ladies that went to that college. I recall one instance where I played (and lost) a game of strip poker in mixed company and desired sex with one of the ladies there that I thought was somewhat attractive and shared a similar name to the same young lady that I had a crush on in junior high and high school. (We'll only say that she had no interest in reciprocating said desires due to others she was personally interested in at the time and leave it at that.)

But there was even one time that were it not for God's hand, grace, and intervention during even my times of wandering as a spiritual prodigal, I honestly wonder what path I might have taken with the rest of my life instead of the path that my God has graciously set me on now. There were a couple of times that I caught one of my roommates in the midst of a sexual act--once with his "fiancee" at the time and another with a young lady that was just a friend to him. The time my roommate had with his "friend", that "friend" also happened to be a young lady that I also had a slight attraction to. My roommate ACTUALLY offered to allow me to have sex with this young lady right then and there plain as day!! You talk about temptation--it stared me right there in the face. I don't know if I hesitated in going through with this because of a simple fear I had in getting that young lady pregnant or God supernaturally preserving my physical virginity (even if I was basically no longer a virgin emotionally, mentally, and psychologically), or BOTH...I just know that if His hand was not on me at the time, my chances for the future enjoyment and fulfillment of having sex with whoever my future bride might be (which, as I write this, I have STILL not been allowed by my God as of yet to be able to enjoy) even more diminished and my image of women even more distorted than it already has been.

So please understand that, as I write this, I am NOT throwing stones at you for what you do. In fact, how DARE I even think of throwing stones at you on this when this is an activity I have engaged in myself? This IS hard for me to reveal this--can you NOT tell already? It grieves me now as I look back at my own past that I at one time sunk to such lows and that I even now still feel its affects.

But for now, let's leave that little past episode and allow me to talk about something that might be less emotionally draining for me. Another perspective that I can look at this from is as one who is involved in some way with the business of mass communications. In one of the basic courses I took in the area of mass communications, we learned about what is known as the "Bradley model of communication". This is one way in which someone can see the process of how people, businesses, etc. communicate with each other. This is how one might diagram it:

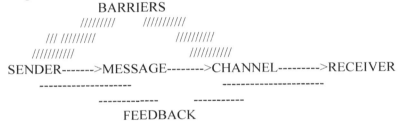

In otherwords, someone has to send a message through some medium (whether it be TV, a newspaper, or some other way) to tell the receiver what the sender wants to say.

But in this process of communication, there will ALWAYS be problems that will prevent the receiver of the message from getting the EXACT message that the sender wished to send in the EXACT manner that the sender meant or intended to send it. For instance, you probably noticed in this model that there are barriers to ANY sort of communication. You might even see this yourself in your own life. What do you think some of those barriers might be?

ANSWER: Some examples might include:

(1.) The meaning of the words that are included in the message by the sender
(2.) Problems on the part of the sender in creating that message in a way the receiver can easily grasp or understand
(3.) Problems that might occur in the process of the delivery of the message by the receiver
(4.) The perception of the receiver of that message may have about the message sent by the sender

How does that sender know for sure whether the receiver got the message he/she wrote, understands it clearly, and responds in the way that the sender would desire to happen? Sometimes, the ONLY way the sender can find out is if that receiver contributes FEEDBACK to the sender about the message sent. What might be some types of FEEDBACK that could be sent back to the original sender?

ANSWER: Possible examples of feedback might include:
(1.) An acknowledgement that the receiver got the message provided by the sender
(2.) A request by the receiver to the sender for further clarification on something in the message
(3.) A subsequent action by the receiver (either positive or negative) that demonstrates to the sender the receiver's response to the sender's message

What does this stuff have to do with pornography, etc.? My answer is A LOT! From my past work in the area of magazine merchandising and in various mass media, I see this even more clearly through my previous work in this field. The aim of magazine publishers (and, if you wished to expand it further, ANYONE involved in the process of selling a newspaper, TV commercial, etc.) is to obviously sell LOTS AND LOTS of magazines and other items so that they can make MONEY!! It's that simple--that's the main objective of it all. But in order to do it, they naturally have to make that product as appealing as possible so that the customer will desire to buy that product and to do it WITHOUT DELAY! Why else do you think publishers try to capitalize on BIG events such as the deaths of Princess Di and Dale Earnhardt? I can tell you this--it's DEFINITELY NOT because they ONLY think that it's a "public service". They simply want the most people buying their magazines (just like any other retailer) that they possibly can and they are usually willing to do whatever it takes to convince you to spend that extra dollar or two that you might prefer to spend on something else instead on THEIR product.

Now let's take that analogy one step further. Now why do you think most men might buy a pornographic magazine or view inappropriate explicit material? Why might some guy opt to buy a Playboy or Penthouse? I can tell you one thing--it's definitely NOT usually for the articles. We'll get into the differences between men and women in a later lesson--but for now, let's take a quick look at what men might buy versus what women might tend to buy. What would you imagine the types of magazines that a young teenage girl might buy? I would doubt seriously that ones on motorcycles or cars might be on the top or bottom of their lists. Usually, they would tend to buy stuff written towards their particular age group such as Teen, Tiger Beat, etc. that might have pictures of cute boys that are hunks and that have stories that are oriented towards the preservation of relationships amongst "friends" and in trying to get asked out on a date by a cute boy in class.

Now let's see what adult women might get whenever they go to a magazine stand. What would you guess they might usually get? Nine times out of ten, it would probably be some magazine again geared towards relationships or with trying to deal with family problems or fix something in the home like a quilt or something like that--something that is primarily focused on being a good housewife and mother. (You could even expand that to such things as Architectural Digest or other related magazines that talk about how to BUILD their first or whatever number home as well.)

BUT what would you imagine a MAN usually getting when he buys a magazine? Rare is the man that will buy a cooking or a quilting magazine UNLESS he's doing it on behalf of his wife at home while he's out shopping (that is, if he ever does it at all). Nope--he might be more prone to buy titles that have articles like this: "How to Have Better Sex", "How To Rev Up Your Sex Drive", etc. Bottom line--women go by and are motivated by relationships and romance and security in the home and the comfort of enjoying SPECIAL relationships that ONLY THEY can legitimately enjoy. But men, in contrast, go by what they see--LITERALLY. The motivation of typical males like myself are more visually-oriented and concerned with outward appearance--ESPECIALLY that of an ATTRACTIVE member of the opposite sex.

So why do we men seem to fall into the lie of pornography, lust, and other sexual addictions at an even more alarming rate? Why can't we men truly find more God-ordained, satisfying relationships with BOTH those of our own gender as well as those of the opposite sex? Why are we so compelled to trade the true manhood that our God has designed for us to have for that of the enemy that only proves to be a lie at the end of the road? I wonder if the answer may truly be that we have ALL been blind--and yet the answer is staring us right in the face.

But what might all of this connect with the subjects of domestic violence and sexual assault from a Biblical perspective? AH--THIS is where the discussion gets even more in-depth and interesting from here. If my God has not dissuaded you from these activities through my own personal experience, then maybe these statistics and other statements that might seem at first glance to be completely out on a limb might shock you to reality:

(1.) One study that I have heard about in regards to domestic violence and sexual assault in my own local area says that 95% OF ALL cases that ONE CENTER has dealt with were usually the result of the MAN being the offender!
(2.) A currently growing cause of the breakdown in the communication and the health of marriages (EVEN among, BLEEP FORBID--CHRISTIAN ONES) is the habitual use of pornography by the male partner in that marriage.
(3.) Several notorious serial killers and rapists have personally attributed the use of pornography of some form as playing a major role for their incentive to commit various heinous acts.
(4.) Numerous celebrities (EVEN those in the Christian world) have been caught in adulterous acts and other inappropriate behaviors that have cost them respect, trust, and even the existence of their careers. We have even had in most recent decades one President who was nearly removed from office as a result of various inappropriate sexually-related behaviors.

Is it any wonder why various national figures and organizations such as the American Family Association and Dr. James Dobson have raised such a stink over the past few years about these issues? Why can't men like me and you rise up and do as our God says instead of responding to the messages that our Adversary has been trying to send us? My God has made a way to stand up in the midst of these temptations--**but why aren't we willing to take advantage of it**?

God has given us the IDEAL picture of what marriage and a proper relationship between a MAN and a WOMAN should be like. He has WONDERFULLY and FEARFULLY made us even with sexual desires and passions that if used right AND IN THE MANNER IN WHICH HE INTENDED FOR THEM TO BE USED IN THE FIRST PLACE can be gloriously used to bring honor, praise, love, adoration, and glory unto His Most Holy Name. BUT OUR ENEMY HAS SABOTAGED THIS INHERITANCE TO US IN MANY WAYS!!

FIRST, the Adversary through domestic violence has completely taken away and distorted the relationships that we have had with our parents and that we ideally should have with those of the opposite sex and has turned what could have been homes of peace and refuge into chaotic war zones. The enemy then cleverly used the demon and monster of sexual assault to take away the trust and security we could have had in close, loving, and secure relationships with others and, as a result, has wrecked our future ability to love and get close to in an intimate way with our future spouse and family.

Through pornography, the enemy has presented us with mirages in the desert of models and others that show us the "good life" and the unending fun that we all will have if we engage in fallacio or group sex or in abhorrent practices that are not honorable or pleasing to His Holy Name. Through lust, the Adversary has turned us away from the proper and right desire for SATISFYING relationships with the spouse that God has chosen and approved for us and instead gotten us to focus ONLY on the illusory pleasures of the moment. And if that were not enough, our Adversary to add insult to injury has used all of the above PLUS distortions in our mainstream media to cause our deteriorating behavior to allow us to be receptive to the abhorrent concept of the need to accept, approve, and even shamefully applaud "alternative lifestyles" that were not considered by our God to be healthy for Sodom and Gomorrah back in ancient times AND that in HIS opinion are STILL not considered healthy NOW!!

Part of this course's aim is to attack FIERCELY the ROOT causes of the issues that contribute to the rise in domestic violence and sexual assault. Well, IF THIS AIN'T A ROOT CAUSE, I CAN'T HARDLY FIND ANYTHING ELSE THAT IS!!! MEN--if I could just passionately plead with you and help you see what this thing called pornography is doing to you, your family, and others you love--MAYBE it would incite you and even me to give this thing up and line up according to God's ways! Oh, WOMEN--if, if only if you can get a small hint or clue why we men might have a weakness for this stuff--then maybe YOU could rise up, make us accountable, and force us to treat you and respect you better and see you for the true, unique beauty that my God instilled within you INSTEAD of settling for the CHEAP substitute of a Playboy or foul, tormenting publication and INSPIRE us to form TRUE, RIGHT, and SATISFYING relationships with you. Now let's go back into the Word for a little bit and see what our God truly thinks about this stuff:

DISCUSSION QUESTIONS:
(1.) Take a quick look at Exodus 20:--ESPECIALLY verses 14 and 17. What does it say to YOU today about these issues?

_____

_____

_____

(2.) What might righteous Job contribute to this little
discussion? Read Job 31:9-12.

(3.) What about these verses that follow here? Is there
ANYTHING that each of these portions of Holy Scripture can
add here?
(Read Prov. 6:25; Matthew 5:28; 1 Cor. 10:6; James 4:2!)

(4.) But what should men TRULY think about the WOMEN they
love? What should we be able to say about them instead? (Read
Prov. 31: !) (HINT: This is something that is read by the
husbands in Jewish families over their wives as a BLESSING
during their observance of the Sabbath!)

(5.) BUT WHAT DOES GOD SAY WE SHOULD TRULY THINK ABOUT
INSTEAD OF LUST, PORNOGRAPHY, ETC? (Check out Galatians 5:16-
26.)

(6.) BUT HOW CAN WE STAND AGAINST THESE THINGS? HOW CAN WE
AVOID THESE DESPICABLE, DETESTABLE BEHAVIORS? (Read Ephesians
6:10-20!)

HOMEWORK: Take some time next week to reflect and think about
the following--and then DO IT:
(1.) ANY times in the past that you might have used
pornographic materials and the SPECIFIC REASONS that you used
them
(2.) What attracted you to those materials in the first place
(3.) Possible effects that it may have on you RIGHT NOW and
also in the future AS WELL AS other people you love and
cherish and hold dear (for example, how it may have affected
your treatment and perception of women)
(4.) DEFINITE ACTION STEPS you can take to overcome these
problems in your life and RESOURCES that you can take
advantage of that will help you and minister to you during

the process of recovering from these addictions

CONCLUSION: Note that this lesson WAS NOT designed to CURE ANYONE of a sexual addiction or inappropriate sexual behaviors BY ANY MEANS!! I HIGHLY RECOMMEND that those seeking deliverance and treatment for more serious problems seek QUALIFIED professional help and take advantage of a number of growing Christian resources now currently available. But I do hope that this at least gives a short surface review of these issues and how it might contribute to the further escalations of instances of domestic violence and sexual assault that are in our society today.

BUT above all, I hope this has made those who have been impacted in ANY WAY by lust, pornography, etc. the DETAILED connections that each of these had with each other. GENTLEMEN--FLEE THESE THINGS FASTER LIKE FOXES ON THE RUN!! Your wives (or future brides--whatever the case may be) DESERVE to be thought of as the ONLY WOMAN that you will EVER love in a special, intimate way! Lust, pornography, etc. hinders your own ability to see a woman the way that GOD would desire for you to see her! DON'T FALL VICTIM OR PREY to this deception and trick of the media!

ALSO--PLEASE understand that lust, etc. DOES NOT JUST COME in the form of a Playboy bunny! I myself have had particular problems in lusting over attractive women in of all things EVENING GOWNS, business dresses, nicely tailored pantsuits, and bridal gowns. Our Savior Himself MAGNIFIED the law when He said that to even LUST after a woman was the same as committing adultery with her in your heart. She was created by God for you to be an absolute compliment and decoration and attractive enhancement and enrichment in your life--NOT AS A PIECE OF MEAT!! THEREFORE, TREAT HER APPROPRIATELY!!

LADIES--be aware why a man is attracted to this stuff. I REFUSE to get on you and say things like "...Well, if you had done so-and-so or hadn't done so-and-so, you wouldn't have been raped (beaten, etc)." THAT IS NOT MY JOB HERE!! AND LET ME BE BLUNT ABOUT THIS--YOU DO NOT DESERVE THE TREATMENT US MEN HAVE GIVEN YOU IN THE PAST! YOU DO NOT DESERVE TO BE TREATED AS A DOORMAT! INSTEAD, my God has placed VERY high value on you and your life. IN FACT--He placed SO HIGH A VALUE ON YOU that His ONLY Son (who also, by the way, happens to be a VERY rich Jewish bridegroom) DIED AND GAVE HIS LIFE JUST FOR YOU! He has been DYING for millennia to reach you and to SWEEP you away into His arms and rapture you for the BIGGEST wedding party of YOUR LIFE!! (We'll go a bit more in regards to the Jewish wedding thing later on, too!)

The Adversary WOULD LOVE to deceive you into thinking that sex is a perverted thing and that it is dirty. But if you would ever venture sometime to take a quick look at the WHOLE book of the Song of Solomon (P.S.--it's somewhere in the Old Testament between Ecclesiastes and Isaiah...)--my God would LOVE to say something TOTALLY and RADICALLY different to you today! God allowed this book to be within the pages of Holy Scripture for a reason. And that was to show what TRUE LOVE between a man and a woman when GOD is the THIRD party to the marriage can really be! Forget those Harloquin, Silhouette, or whatever romance novels you might be reading now--AND INSTEAD, pick up the very Word of God for YOURSELF and see how the King of Kings and Lord of Lords has decided to write HIS romance novel! I can almost guarantee that it will change your view of romance FOREVER! Give praise unto our God for this revelation--for He is good and His mercy endures forever!

TO ALL: Remember that ALL THAT REALLY GLITTERS IS NOT GOLD!! ONLY GOD can satisfy those deep longings and passions you may have! ONLY GOD can fill those empty spaces and holes that you may have! NO pornographic materials or cheap, lousy substitutes can replace the beauty and majesty of a covenant relationship between a man, a woman, and God in the way HE has ordained it--NOT US!! Don't let these lustful thoughts, inappropriate materials, or other things keep you away from your relationship with God and an enjoyable, satisfying relationship with your future spouse. Don't be deceived by the fool's gold of fleeting images that will not satisfy for long--be satisfied simply instead by the thoughts and plans my God has for you. " "'For I know the plans I have for you,' declares the LORD, '...plans to prosper you and not to harm you, plans to give you hope and a future.'" (Jeremiah 29:11)

PRAYER: Creator Father, God Almighty, and Lord Jesus/Y'shua:
Thank you for teaching me today about being careful to realize that all that really glitters is not gold when it comes to appearances and the evil that can come in various forms. Help me to shun those things that are not of you, to avoid certain lusts and things that are not right and proper for me to pursue, and instead replace them ONLY with thoughts that are beautiful and that are of You. Help me to also change my perception and view of the opposite sex from the distortion my Adversary has given me to that which lines up with that which you've said in your Word. Help me to NOT believe everything that I see in the media about women, but INSTEAD to confess and think about ONLY what you have to say about them and to think ONLY pure thoughts about them. I thank you and give you praise, thanks, and honor in the

name of your Son, Y'shua Ha'Meshiach/the Lord Jesus Christ--AMEN!!

UNIT II, LESSON 2--"He Sent Her Flowers Only Once": What The Monster of Sexual Assault REALLY Looks Like

[AUTHOR'S NOTE: Some of the materials talked about in the chapter that follows will unfortunately be necessarily sexually explicit and graphic in nature. THEREFORE--It is the recommendation of this author that young children and sensitive readers not read any further than this notice and proceed on to other less explicit chapters of this book.]

I was privileged one time to have the opportunity to assist a certain man who is highly involved in the area of prison ministry crusades and evangelistic events. This minister, an older man that was a major influence on the creation of his ministry, and myself were heading towards a couple of state prison units in Pampa, TX to do a weekend crusade. It's amazing, though, how our God can even cause ministry opportunities to pop up when you least expect them.

We had stopped at a truck stop in Amarillo to take a quick restroom break and get a snack or two before moving on. I had just gotten outside when I realized that there was a book that I had recently gotten that I had brought along with me to show them and was about to ask him to open the trunk of his minivan so that I could get it. Just as I was about to ask him, I found him talking to this lady in at first what appeared to be casual conversation, but in then what turned to be a bit of intense ministry that he was providing the lady.

It just so happened that she was traveling across the country with her husband (who happened to be a truck driver himself) and son. And overhearing this lady talk just about broke my heart--ESPECIALLY when she started telling my friend about how she was suffering from both verbal and physical abuse from her husband. In fact, if she had the notion, she probably would have gotten her son and went into the minivan with us to get herself some help.

Thankfully, my friend realized in some way that if she did this (thankfully, her husband was in the truck sleeping at the time), the three of us would be, to say the least, in a really big speck of trouble. He prayed for her first about this situation--then I somehow felt led to ask her if she had also been sexually abused as well. She then said yes to that question--to which I then added a prayer that God would Himself reach down and truly embrace her with his love. After this was over with, I suggested a couple of places that I was aware of in Amarillo that I thought might be of help to her in her current situation--and my friend also wisely suggested to her that first she should call 911 and talk to the police. We also gave her some literature that she could take with her--some of which my friend had on hand as well as a copy of Joyce Meyer's ministry magazine that I had in a bag that I was planning to give to one of the chaplains of the prison units we were heading to. She thanked us for the help and counsel--and the three of us in the minivan continued on our journey northward.

In reflecting over this recent experience, I couldn't help but think of a couple of incidents that happened in my prior upbringing and experience that probably illustrates better than anything else the difference between common myths that people have about the proper boundaries (sexual and otherwise) that men and women should have with each other, what rape and sexual assault is truly all about, and what the real causes of this are.

Being a man that (as of this writing, at least) has not been given the blessing and privilege of a more intimate relationship with someone of the opposite sex, my mind is probably more personally attuned to most the physical and sexual desires and the natural need to desire intimate companionship with a young lady that might eventually lead to marriage. I recall (as was referred to in the previous chapter) how when I was growing up through both junior high and high school that I had a MAJOR crush and infatuation with one of the girls that was in the same grade and classes that I was in. And this wasn't just a quick fling, either--I recall that I was quite smitten with her.

You would not believe the attempts I made to try to convince her of the merits of being MY girlfriend. I even, when I heard one time that she and an older boy that was her current "boyfriend" at the time had broken up, I even asked him if I could, in a sense, take over his place (to which he chivalously consented). Apparently, though, the young lady did not acknowledge this little claim or reciprocate with any
obvious desire and affection for me on her part. I tried giving her flowers and even a ring with her birthstone on it--but no dice, for she would not bulge even an inch. She apparently had her own desires set on a boy who was a senior--who she apparently dated for a year or two before he moved on to another girl a grade ahead of her. Needless to say, this young lady taught me through her example just what romance should and should NOT be. The major rule above all else that she taught me? It definitely takes two to tango. If one party doesn't consent to do something, then nothing else is able to legitimately happen. And my puppy love for this young lady went forever unrequited. (Ah, well...)

43

Now we'll fast forward a number of years to an incident that happened when I was in junior college. (Note: This was during the period of what I personally consider my version of the wild and woolier years of my life.) I had went with a group of honor students to the national convention of the honor society that I was a member of that was being held that year in Washington, D.C. During one night of the convention, there was a dance that was held at a place near the hotel that the convention was going on at.

I recall quite well meeting a young lady who was very physically attractive and actually seemed to be quite friendly with me, was quite uninhibited (shall we say), and seemed to desire a little physical closeness with me on the dance floor. There was one itsy bitsy problem with her--she was drunk as a skunk at the time. How can I tell that she was drunk? Actually, it was quite simple. When I even lightly twirled her around while we were dancing, she immediately went head first into the floor. I really felt sorry for her at the time and was actually a bit worried and concerned for her. She was making moves up and down my body that would have made some of the dances that Patrick Swayze and his lady friend dance partner made in "Dirty Dancing" seem like a G-rated Disney movie. If I had not tried to be a proper gentleman at the time, I feared that the temptation to take advantage of her within her drunken stupor would have been too great and resulted in some very regretable circumstances for the both of us. I was sad, in a way, when her friends came to take her back to her room--but quite relieved for her sake when they decided that it might be a good idea to send her to bed a little early.

You're obviously wondering what the above stories have to do with sexual assault and rape. You would be surprised, though, to find that these are actually some of the most common scenarios that people may tend to think of when it comes to crimes of a sexual nature. Unfortunately, these are also ideas that actually lead to some of the common misconceptions that most people have (even within Christ's church) about these issues. Therefore, the purpose of this chapter is to explore a bit more detail the misconceptions of the origins of sexual assault and rape, the preconceived ideas that some might have into whose fault the crimes ultimately lie, what the truth REALLY is about these issues, and (more importantly) what the Word of God has to say about these things.

First, let's go into brief definitions of what the terms "sexual assault" and "rape" are. The booklet "Rape and Rape Trauma Syndrome" defines these terms as follows:

Sexual assault: An act of violence against another WITHOUT consent for sexual assault

Rape: Forced sexual intercourse against a person's will; a hostile, violent assault that persons commit to dominate, overpower, and humiliate other persons

Maybe to get a better picture of what these two monsters are all about, it might be as good of a time as any to start our Discussion Questions for this section:

DISCUSSION QUESTIONS:

(I.) Fill out the following "Rape Myth Acceptance Scale" worksheet:

For the statements which follow, please circle the number that best indicates your opinion--what you believe. If you strongly disagree, you would answer "1"; if you strongly agree, you would answer "7". If you feel neutral, you would answer "4"--and so on.

1--disagree strongly
2--disagree somewhat
3--disagree slightly
4--neutral
5--agree slightly
6--agree somewhat
7--agree strongly

_____ (1.) A woman who goes to the home or apartment of a man on their first date implies that she is willing to have sex.
_____ (2.) Any female can get raped.
_____ (3.) One reason that women falsely report a rape is that they frequently have a need to call attention to themselves.
_____ (4.) Any healthy woman can successfully resist a rapist if she really wants to.
_____ (5.) When women go around braless or wearing short skirts or tight tops, they are just asking for trouble.
_____ (6.) Women who get raped while hitchhiking get what

they deserve.

_____ (7.) A woman who is stuck up and thinks she is too good to talk to guys on the street deserves to be taught a lesson.

_____ (8.) Many woman have an unconscious wish to be raped, and may then unconsciously set up a situation in which they are likely to be attacked.

_____ (9.) If a woman gets drunk at a party and has intercourse with a man she's just met there, she should be considered "fair game" to other males at the party who want to have sex with her, too--whether she wants to or not.

_____ (10.) In the majority of rapes, the victim is promiscuous or has a bad reputation.

_____ (11.) If a girl engages in necking or petting and she lets things get out of hand, it is her own fault if her partner forces sex on her.

Please use the following key to answer the next two questions:

1--Almost none
2--A few
3--Some
4--About half
5--Many
6--A lot
7--Almost all

Write the number that shows what fraction you believe to be true.

_____ 12. What percentage of women who report a rape would you say are lying because they are angry and want to get back at the man they accuse?

_____ 13. What percentage of reported rapes would you guess were merely invented by women who discovered they were pregnant and wanted to protect their own reputation?

Please use the following key to answer the following questions:

1--Never
2--Rarely
3--Sometimes
4--Half the time
5--Often
6--Usually
7--Always

A person comes to you and claims they were raped. How likely would you be to believe their statement if the person were:

_____ 14. Your best friend?

_____ 15. An Indian woman?

_____ 16. A neighborhood woman?

_____ 17. A young boy?

_____ 18. A Black woman?

_____ 19. A white woman?

_____

(II.) Take the following test of your knowledge about the myths and facts about rape and sexual assault (based on the outline of the video series "Help...I've Been Raped: What You Need to Know About Investigating Sexual Assaults of Women"):

(1.) Multiple Choice: Sexual assault is--
(a.) A crime of aggression, dominance, and control
(b.) Perpetuated without consent
(c.) Something that occurs in a relationship as a matter of power and control
(d.) Strips a person of all dignity
(e.) The most degrading, brutalizing thing to do to a person other than murder

(f.) Something that makes those who do rape feel a sense of entitlement to sex by the person violated
(g.) None of the above
(h.) ALL of the above

(2.) Fill in the Blanks/Essay:
(a.) What is the ratio of the number of sexual assaults not reported to the authorities? _____

(b.) Give three reasons why sexual assault tends to go unreported:
(1.) _____
(2.) _____
(3.) _____

(c.) What, according to the statistics of one facility that works with sexual assault, are the MOST COMMON clothes that anyone who is raped and/or sexually assaulted?
_____

(d.) _____ out of _____ women will be sexually assaulted in her lifetime. Out of those, _____ out of every _____ report the crime.

(e.) These are the percentages of who usually commit the crime of rape: _____ acquaintances/friends/relatives and or those closest to them; _____ strangers.

(f.) Even if sexual assault is the least prosecuted crime in Texas and other states, why should we still pursue those cases?
_____
_____
_____
_____

(III.) MYTHS AND FACTS:
Answer the following as either being a myth (M) or a fact (F) about sexual assault:

_____ (1.) The victim probably did something to deserve the rape/sexual assault.

48

_____ (2.) Well--only beautiful, sexy women are raped. She got what she deserved by being born with good looks. A man just can't control himself around someone like her. She's asking for it.

_____ (3.) It's okay to sexually assault another person. Not all people are equal, you know.

_____ (4.) As long as you blame the victim, you'll never know the truth about a sexual assault.

_____ (5.) Well, a male officer just can't handle a sexual assault case. Only a woman officer can take care of cases involving women.

_____ (6.) Sexual assault not only causes physical damage, but also scars the soul as well.

_____ (7.) PROVEN effects of the aftermath of a sexual assault (whether it occurred as a child or as an adult) can possibly include:
_____ (a.) Suicide?
_____ (b.) Drug/alcohol abuse?
_____ (c.) Pregnancy?
_____ (d.) A tendency towards lesbianism/homosexuality?
_____ (e.) Distrust of those of the opposite sex?
_____ (f.) Increased problems with submission and obedience to APPROPRIATE authority?
_____ (g.) Increased chances for future incarceration?
_____ (h.) Bitterness and hatred?
_____ (i.) Desires for vengeance against the assailant in a manner that is not lawful and not constructive?

_____ (8.) The treatment of the victim by the first responding officers and other caring individuals at the scene can make a significant different in the successful prosecution of a case.

_____ (9.) Only women can be raped or sexually assaulted. There's no possible or conceivable way that a man or a young child can be sexually abused or taken advantage of.

(IV.) BUT WHAT DOES HOLY SCRIPTURE TEACH IN REGARDS TO RAPE AND SEXUAL ASSAULT?

(a.) There are AT LEAST TWO major places in the Word of God in which a sexual assault not only caused problems for the victim herself, BUT ALSO for many more people as well.

 (1.) Read Gen. 34: and what it says about Dinah and the Shechemites. What happened to Dinah in this passage? What did Shechem, son of Hamor, decide to do in response? What was the reaction of the sons of Israel to Shechem's offer? Did Shechem agree to the terms the sons of Israel required in order for him to obtain Dinah as his wife? And what were the tragic consequences of it all?

 (2.) What about 2 Sam. 13: and the things that happened between Amnon and Tamor? Why did this happen in the first place? What was Absalom's reaction when Tamor told him about what Amnon had done to her? What was King David's reaction to the incident? What did Absalom decide to finally do to Amnon to avenge what Amnon had done to Tamor? What were the eventual results and consequences of it all for everyone concerned. (Continue reading further through chapter 19 to get "...the rest of the story".)

(b.) What do the following Old Testament scriptures show about rape: Isa. 13:16; Lamentations 5:11; Zechariah 14:2?

(c.) What might God's response to those who have been considered guilty of rape? Read Deuteronomy 22:25.

(d.) BUT HOW DOES GOD TRULY VIEW SEX?
   (1.) Where does God think sex truly belongs? (Heb. 13:4; Matt. 19:4-6; Mark 10:1-12)
   (2.) How might God view those who commit sins of rape and sexual assault? (1 Cor. 6:9-20)

(3.) How important is marriage in regards to our relationship with Him? (Eph. 5:22-33) Is a person who sexually assaults another defiling God's true purposes for sex, marriage, and family and therefore guilty of sin against Him?

(4.) Is God the Creator of sex? Is it a dirty and shameful thing to Him--or did He bless and honor and sanctify it and proclaim it to be good and right within proper and appropriate boundaries? (Gen. 1:26-28 AND 2:20a-25) Did God pervert sex--or did someone or something else do it?

(5.) Take a quick look at the entirety of the whole book of the Song of Solomon. What does the WHOLE book say about what God thinks sex should truly be?

I think the comments that the Promise Keepers Men's Study Bible notes about Song of Solomon 5:1 and 7:1-13 are quite excellent in pointing out what God's true view of sex is better than anything else I can think of:

(5:1) "If you've ever wondered how God feels about sexual intimacy, no verse in the Bible declares God's attitude toward it more clearly than this one...

"...Understanding the passage requires reflecting on what has led up to it. During their wedding night, Solomon tenderly praised his bride (4:1-7). Then he calmed her fearful thoughts (4:8) and they began to make love (4:9-11). Finally, through tender imagery provided by the garden metaphor, we read that they consummated their marriage (4:12-5:1). The friends respond in celebration of this relationship--this is sexuality as it is meant to be expressed. The fact that this passage appears in God's Word is a sign of divine approval for the sexual pleasure Solomon and his bride gave and received.

"...Today, this beautiful, God-ordained activity has been distorted. Many men feel a sense of guilt about their sexual urges because what they see and hear and read about is so far removed from God's original design. Since that kind of sexual activity draws God's disapproval, it can be easy for us to think that God disapproves of all sexual activity. Nothing could be further from the truth--the same God who designed humans as sexual creatures endorses sex within the confines of marriage..."

In referring to S of S 7:1-13, the PK Men's Study Bible gives three major points that sum up best what God's overall total view of sex is throughout Holy Scripture:

(1.) Sex is GOD'S idea!
(2.) God designed sex to be pleasurable.
(3.) Sexual expression within marriage is a preventative to sexual infidelity outside of marriage.

The Oxford Companion to the Bible (p. 690-692) further adds this as far as how the Bible defined the purposes of marriage and sex:

(1.) Social (the regulation of sexual behavior, especially of women)
(2.) Psychological and emotional (to provide companionship for the partners)
(3.) Economic (through family agrarian and artisan enterprises)
(4.) Religious (since the majority of festivals centered on household participation)
(5.) Theological (through the procreation, legitimization, and socialization of children, the basis of the people of God)

I think based on the evidence presented above, I would hardly see what benefit (if any at all) that the decision of someone to rape someone else would have. IN FACT-- it only leads to intense and unimaginable pain that causes nothing but sorrow, heartache, and absolute devastation and destruction all around. BUT DON'T BLAME GOD FOR THIS--FOR IT IS NOT HIS FAULT!! He didn't plan for this rape or assault to happen--NO, MA'AM...NO, SIR!! The Savior Himself points out who is the real enemy in John 10:10: "The thief comes only to steal, kill, and destroy; I have come that they may have life, and have it to the full." Those of you who have been forced to become victims of this hideous crime--I tenderly beg and plead for you to realize that God DID NOT put this on you. NO--God wants you to know that you are VERY special and treasured by Him, the Ruler of the Universe Himself. And this Abba Father desperately longs to show you that you are a valuable daughter or son of His. God NEVER PERVERTS SEX--it's the one who decided to rebel against Him that does.

Yes, it may have been a man you thought you trusted that completely tore your world apart by this cowardly act--but rest assured that it was satan himself...yes, even the old Adversary himself, that was ultimately influencing and cheerleading the one who butchered you and tore your dignity and soul into shreds by forcing you into an heinous act in which only death could be much worse. He does NOT want you to enjoy sex (ESPECIALLY in marriage--whether you are in one now or hope someday to be married).

BUT MY GOD WANTS TO SAY TO YOU--IT'S NOT YOUR FAULT!! You did not do anything to deserve this and, as far as He is concerned, you were the one who was truly wronged in His eyes. And He HAS promised to be your Shield, Defender, Guardian, and Stay. He will avenge on your behalf what has been done to you--for He is THE Righteous Judge of the Universe. And (unlike the courts that man presides over) He will see to it somewhere down the line that those who hurt you will be properly and fairly judged for those deeds.

In God's eyes, ANY perversion such as rape and sexual assault that anyone does against His ways and in manners that get in the way of His very unique plan for marriage (especially in relation to a woman) is HIGHLY OFFENSIVE to the nostrils of God and breaks His heart terribly. And to those victims who have suffered this horrible offense, His heart is VERY broken over you and He DESPERATELY desires to shelter you under His wings and tell you that everything will be all right in HIS due time if you will simply rest in Him. He DOES NOT promise you rose gardens or flowers as you try to pick up the pieces from this situation. But more than ever, He wants to be the true and loving Bridegroom and Husband who tenderly desires to love and protect you with all His might--NOT to rape, attack, or humiliate you. (Isa. 54:5; Rev. 19:7). And let Him use others that will also demonstrate His grace and love in ways that you've never imagined before!

[HOMEWORK:] In your mind, roleplay a situation involving rape or sexual assault. Then, ask yourself the following questions:

(a.) What thoughts might be going through the victim's mind
in this process?
(b.) What about the perpetrator?
(c.) What might GOD possibly want to say to both involved in
this situation?

PRAYER: Abba Father--thank You for Your reassurance that even in the most traumatic situations that I have suffered that You still love and care for me and have my best interests at heart. Help me to have Your eyes to see the person who put me in this unfortunate situation the way You see them in spite of whatever pain they may have caused me. And help me in due time to be able to treat them as You would treat them. But for now until that time comes, shelter me in the meantime under the ultimate shelter of Your wings and help me to heal and pick up the pieces of my life which is now sadly shattered. And most of all--even in the worst of situations, help me to still praise You and have a song in my heart for all that You already HAVE done and will CONTINUE to do for me and others. In your Son's name--Amen.

UNIT II, LESSON III--INDEPENDENCE DAY FOR CINDERELLA AND PRINCE CHARMING

In talking about what we are fixing to think about and discuss for a little while in this lesson, there's a song called "Independence Day" by country artist Martina McBride in which I wish I knew the exact words to, but can't necessarily think of what they are at the time that I write this. But I think the title is extremely appropriate here. I recall watching the video of this many times and listening to the music of this and the theme that plays throughout the presentation of the effects of domestic violence on both a family and a community. The uncontrollable rage of a husband, the abject desperation of a wife unsure how to get herself out of the trap she finds herself in, the children caught in the middle by forces that are completely out of their control, and a community completely bumfuzzled on what to do about the whole situation. All of this becoming a scene of sheer tragedy--a tragedy that could have been easily prevented.

But not all the things that domestic violence does garner that much publicity. There are instances, for example, that I know of personally that might show you more aptly that there are ways that this scourge--THIS HORRIFIC MONSTER--can affect the lives of people many years after these incidents. Unfortunately, to these people who still suffer the unfortunate consequences, it seems all too normal and real--and it is hard to see things going any other way for them.

But the saddest indictment of all is probably what I fear has befallen the Body of Christ in regards to these serious issues. I'm sorry to get too much on my soapbox here against those who claim to be Christians--BUT MY PASSIONATE ANGER AND RAGE LITERALLY BURNS INSIDE MY SPIRIT TOWARDS THIS ISSUES AND I WILL NOT KEEP SILENT ANY LONGER!!!!!!!!!!!!!! In regards to this silent holocaust of the heart, I REFUSE to have to stand before my God and be accountable to Him for not speaking the truth in these issues and exposing evil where it may deeply reside.

My charge against the Body of Christ is unfortunately this--while lives have literally been destroyed physically, emotionally, and spiritually by this disgusting, repulsive carcass of a demon, the Body of Christ (at least in those parts of it which I am aware of) has in essence abrogated its duty to deal with EVERYONE affected by these issues and at best has been AWOL in their duties and responsibilities to these folks. But worse yet is the sad fact that there are various churches within the Body that have willingly or unwillingly served as an unwitting co-conspirator in this hideous spiritual attack by the enemy. And we are forced to pay prices for all of this in many ways.

Let's take an example or two from my past experiences in assisting various prison ministries to get a clearer picture of what I mean. I had an opportunity to assist an older man in a certain men's group with a 10-week men's Bible study within one of the state prison units near where I live. There was a time or two where it seemed that I had an occasion or two during this period of time where I was able to hopefully contribute a lesson of some substance given to me by my God that might make a difference in their lives.

During one of these times with this group, I in essence started teaching a lesson on how all of us should view the various roles and functions within the greater Church. I focused the discussion on passages in 1 Timothy as well as in Titus and even found a way to incorporate my love of chess as a way to give the men (whom most of them may have possibly had problems understanding through reading text; but could see the point better through a more visual demonstration) a practical way to visually see how different people playing different roles contribute to the overall operation of the Body of Christ.

In the course of this discussion, I asked the men of what they saw and thought the role of women should be both in society and in the Church. The answers each of them gave in general disappointed and shocked me--and almost broke my heart. Here I am a typical man--and yet I was discussing the role of women...and no woman was able to be present to tell them what SHE truly felt her proper place should be in comparison to a man.

The consensus responses of the men present? The majority basically gave her almost no role at all EXCEPT for her to be barefoot and pregnant and to be no more than the equivalent of a glorified housekeeper. This sadly revealed to me what major problems of perception face those who are offenders both behind bars as well as those just released. They just could not see that a woman has just as much value to our God (if not more so to a man) as they do. It definitely opened my eyes in seeing how much they so desperately needed to learn about these subjects and how our Adversary has done a very good job of deception in the area of how our women should be treated by a man.

But the lights began to come on in terms of personal revelation about the problems in our prisons once I found something else out--especially in regards to the scourge of domestic violence. Another night, I was able to get a ride back with another one of my fellow volunteers back to my apartment. This man and wife also happened to serve as one of the "volunteer chaplains" of one of our local area's state prison units and (as part of those duties) also headed an anger management class on that unit. On the way back home, I asked them both two questions just out of curiosity (because at the time I was myself thinking a lot about the issues of domestic violence and sexual assault through various other training that I was undergoing at the time). I asked them, "I want to know two things. In your anger management group, I'd like to know: first--how many of those men in that group have been involved in some way with domestic violence, whether they were a batterer themselves and/or were abused as a child? And second--how many of those men in that same group have been involved in any way with sexual assault?" [Before I give you that answer, I do need to let you know that the particular unit this is referring to was at the time what is considered in my state a prison facility specifically designated for the treatment of probationers dealing with substance-abuse problems.]

The answers of that couple to my questions nearly threw me back for a loop. The man said that at least 65% of the men in that group have been batterers themselves. But that was nothing compared to the statistic that he gave for sexual assault. He further said that 90%--folks, that is NINETY percent, NINE-ZERO--that were at minimum at least sexually molested or abused as a child. From this, it became quite obvious to me why our criminal justice system in our nation has been a total failure in the area of recidivism. Through this, I realized that we cannot expect to solve the problems of our system UNLESS we first in the Body of Christ wake up to the knowledge that we must help those that have suffered with these devastating problems resolve these unfinished issues of their childhood before we can even expect them to begin the long journey that they must take to become productive citizens.

I did not want to go into a ministry of this nature AT ALL!! I made the decision to work to tackle these issues ONLY after a great amount of time and training, prayer (and even a little fasting to boot), searching the Scriptures, and seeking His will to see if this is where He truly wanted me to go. If it were up to me, I would NOT take this burden on--but would instead be happy and content with life in the music industry and being free and single.

But after what I have seen and heard and experienced personally, I cannot honestly dare attempt anything else that might be of greater service to my Savior. Not when I literally see a silent holocaust of men, women, and children who have never heard the message of a loving Father and Son begging and pleading for them to accept their free and unmerited gift of salvation...all because they could not accept the fact of the

Father's love due to the simple, heartbreaking fact that they have no idea of what a loving father is like in the first place. If we in the Body of Christ will not dare stand up and offer what is an infinitely superior solution to the root causes of our problems, then we are definitely of no earthly good or value to His Holy Name.

I think, therefore, that it is time for us in the Body of Christ to, in essence, on the behalf of those who are suffering from these horrific scourges of the heart to declare today as Independence Day for Cinderella and Prince Charming. Why, though, is this necessary? Because the fairy tales our Adversary has been trying to tell us is simply a bunch of bold-faced lies--and Christ's Message is the ONLY thing that can ultimately stand as the pure truth needed to counteract the mirage of this fairy tale. Only the Gospel of our Lord that is pure, undefiled, and truly preached can set our Cinderellas and Prince Charmings free from this beast that threatens to tear them, their children, and our society apart. And all because we in the Body have not done our part to take care of the root problems and causes that have destroyed these trees of promise.

The problem, though, in this process is the fact, as the prophet Hosea said--"...my people are destroyed from lack of knowledge." (Hos. 4:6, NIV) But, in my opinion, ignorance is DEFINITELY NOT bliss in this situation. And only in the impartation of appropriate revelation and knowledge and the destruction of ignorance in regards to these issues will all of us be truly free in the future from this scourge called domestic violence.

Some people in Christian circles may discount the opinions of those that may not exactly share their faith [(Ex.) Psychologists and social workers], but who do at least demonstrate some form of competence in regards to their knowledge and understanding of these issues I at least feel should be accorded a proper opportunity to let their voices be heard as a part of this discussion. This is NOT intended to be by ANY means a comprehensive covering of this particular topic--but only at best a brief overview that will at least attempt to cover some important major points and line them up and back them with evidence from God's Word that will serve as further reinforcement of these points and also provide an impetus for further detailed individual study towards these particular issues--especially in how God might view these in light of His will and His Word.

I recently found that the work of Norm Nickle, MSW, through his video "Ending Family Violence: Dynamics of Abuse" in regards to this topic a beneficial way that might give all of us a very brief overview to see what this monster of domestic violence looks like inside and out. Let's stop for a while and examine his thoughts and see if we can find how his statements and theories might line up with Holy Scripture.

Nickle cites five overall powerful dynamics of domestic violence that are most common in these situations:

(1.) Violence as a learned behavior modeled at an early age
(2.) Abuse as a learned method of dealing with stress
(3.) Use of anger to mask primary feelings
(4.) Unrealistic expectations of relationships
(5.) Gender warfare

First, let me address the Body of Christ for just a quick second. Most of our people when it comes to seeing these situations automatically assume that the victim, drugs, or alcohol (or something like that) had something to do with the violent reaction of the offender. Nickle, though, attempts to attack that notion head on by saying that domestic violence is the decision of ONE PERSON ONLY--THE OFFENDER!! ONLY the offender himself can and must decide to end the violence first and then learn to control his anger.

Now, let's deal with the second dynamic that Nickle talks about. Nickle as a part of this also cites what he considers four "styles of explosion" that might be prevalent in an abusive person:

(1.) Buildup/Explosion/Remorse (which Nickle feels is the most common cycle of most offenders in terms of how each deals with how each controls stress and deals with anger; men with this tendency will try not to deal with the anger while the woman who wants to encourage the man to talk about it are considered by the man to be an intrusion; man will eventually explode, usually over something trivial which immediately can lead to a violent act; then man feels remorse for his actions against the victim and attempt to do things that will convince the victim of the abuse to sweep the incident under the rug and lull her to complacency--only for the process to begin all over again)

(2.) During the buildup stage--abuse and intimidation pervade throughout this stage before the explosion with increasingly serious threats and explosions followed by angry silent

withdrawals; the final BIG explosion is simply a culmination
of what has gone before; the remorse stage is mixed with
false tears and promises; offender might blame victim or try
to buy off victim with expensive gifts; suicide threats, etc.
are also common here

(3.) Offender maintains very high level of stress and is
HIGHLY unaware of how tightly wound they are; violence seems
to come out of nowhere; is VERY unpredictable and terrible

(4.) Offender goes through NONE of the stages of the
buildup/explosion/remorse cycle; is usually very cold,
calculating, and pathological; and has NO remorse and NO
desire to change

Nickle says about Dynamic (#3.) that what we might call anger is sometimes instead
the masking of primary emotions that will be eventually converted into anger. He
also says that there are two things that men have particular problems with in regards
to this: (1.) that they don't have the internal vocabulary necessary to be able to say
how they TRULY feel; and (2.) that they don't feel like they have the permission
to talk about and properly vent those feelings in a constructive manner. He also notes
that most abusers are VERY sensitive people who are crying for their feelings to be
acknowledged--but at the same time believe that they would be perceived as being
weak if these feelings were expressed openly. He attributes this to unresolved issues
from the past and that a small incident in the present can trigger some stuff that man
felt as a child.

Meanwhile, victims (CONTRARY to what most believe) NEVER enjoy abuse--and
most DO try to leave or get divorced. But those in the Body of Christ, according to
Nickle, shouldn't be surprised if a women feels compelled to stay in an abusive
situation because of the following reasons:

(1.) Physical [(Ex.) Fear of retaliation by the offender if
the victim attempts to leave]
(2.) Financial [(Ex.) Not being able to support the children
on welfare vs. dealing with what they perceive to be
occasional abuse]
(3.) Fear that the offender will kidnap the kids
(4.) Offender is a good husband and father when not violent

Contrary to what you might believe--they DON'T want to leave their husband...they just want the abuse to stop posthaste in whatever ways possible! Those that wonder why these victims are afraid to seek outside help should now see why they cannot reasonably be expected to take any blame for what has happened or to do things on their own. And offenders--this is why I must be harsher on you than anyone else (NOT out of condemnation, of course--but in true love and concern for your future spiritual growth and well-being)...because if YOU had not been in control, none of this stuff on anyone else's part would have been necessary. Let's put this stuff back on the heads where the blame should truly lie--the person who started the whole thing in the first place and the Prince of the Power of the Air who influenced you to do such a horrific deed!

Before we move further in this lesson, let's take some time to do our DISCUSSION QUESTIONS for this time and work on some PRACTICAL exercises to discover more about our own selves and learn a thing or two of what is involved in the cycle of domestic violence:

DISCUSSION QUESTIONS:

(1.) What are some primary feelings that we might substitute
the word "anger" for? What are terms that we should REALLY
use to tell what are our TRUE FEELINGS AND EMOTIONS ARE?
[Write these down on a piece of paper for future reference.]

(2.) What might be some BAD responses in how you can deal
with your anger? What might be some better ways that you can
do instead to keep that anger in check and in control?

(3.) Let's think about the story of Cinderella and Prince
Charming for a moment or two.
(a.) What are some words or characteristics that we might use
to describe Cinderella?
(b.) How about the same for Prince Charming?
(c.) What about the ugly stepsisters?
(d.) What would we desire to be the final result of it all?
(e.) But what would be the REALISTIC final result of it all?
(f.) How could all of this relate to the problem of domestic
violence?

Nickle tries to show through the above exercises that the solution to the problems mentioned above CANNOT be resolved by getting into a marital relationship. IN FACT, Nickle cites that marriages are BAD places to do therapy because the wife DOES NOT have any idea of what the man really wants and the man cannot realistically coerce his wife to make him happy and fulfill his needs--needs which should have been resolved during his childhood, but weren't for one reason or another. The result? This becomes the PERFECT formula for the destruction of a marriage. And Nickle notes that 85% of the marriage counseling work he has done involves couples who suffer from these unrealistic expectations.

But what was even more compelling for me was when I came to another realization of something I wrote earlier in this book--and it didn't come to me until AFTER it was confirmed by my viewing of Nickle's video. Remember the "Tribal Initiation" that we did to start this course of study? I originally read about this from a book written by a United Church of Christ minister named Gordon Dalbey called "Healing The Masculine Soul".

In his book, Dalbey talks about an instance when he taught in Nigeria and was asked by a student about how we in the West did what could be called a "tribal initiation" that would enable the community to help a boy come out and deal with his adolescent issues and find his place in the world as a man. At first, I didn't really grasp the implications of this strange concept.

But then, remembering my own personal experiences as a son of a single mother and the unique problems I faced without the constant presence of POSITIVE male role models--I eventually came to see the need to incorporate that concept into this book due to both that as well as the numerous things that I was witness to in our prison system. But I couldn't put a good solid foundational basis on the WHY to do this "Tribal Initiation" thing UNTIL I saw the Nickle video. Nickle gives this interesting list of skills that mature men need to know in order to live stable, productive lives:

(1.) Difference between respect and fear
(2.) How to honor the rights and boundaries of others
(3.) How to be vulnerable and self-disclosed
(4.) How to experience criticism without anger
(5.) How to find a calm center within themselves
(6.) How to be intimate without losing your independence
(7.) How to feel genuine pride and self-respect

(8.) How to get support from other men

(9.) How to be passionately alive without being violent

UNFORTUNATELY, offenders have problems obtaining the above skills because of the following (and, therefore, leading to the following results):

(1.) Lack of proper POSITIVE male role models

(2.) Overreliance on "locker room advice" from equally insecure youth

(3.) Belief that power and control is the way to dominate other people

(4.) Offenders never truly learn to love people WITHOUT attempting to control them

(5.) The above inabilities leave BOTH sexes confused and leaves a LOT of room for anger directed at the other sex

Nickle notes that this can easily be described by two stages in the maturity and development in the life of boys and girls:

1ST STAGE--Need to bond CLOSELY with the parent of the opposite gender for nurturing, protection, etc.; Relationship of father to the little girl--THIS IS THE TIME where the father needs to appropriately protect the boundaries! (Usually the time that a girl is more susceptible to molestation, etc. because of her want and need to feel the love of an adult man...) [PROBLEM--Boys usually get this bonding from their moms WHILE girls DON'T get this from their dads!]

2ND STAGE--Occurs around 11 or 12 (or sometime during puberty); opposite sex parent needs to begin letting go and the child needs to break away and bond with a parent or parent figure of the same gender; THIS WILL eventually determine the state of any future relationships the child may have with someone of the opposite sex; this is also the time where the child is seeking appropriate mentoring from figures of the same sex; problems during this particular stage WILL reap DRAMATIC consequences later on in life if this same-sex bonding is not properly done

I could go on and on with this--but probably the summation of what Nickle would say is this (at least in my opinion)...is it any wonder that we still have people in adult bodies who are still acting like Peter Pan and as if "...I don't want to grow up!"? We still have emotionally-scarred people who are ruined because of this domestic violence monster and people who still suffer because of this. And I personally hope that you are not one of them!!

IF YOU ARE ANY participant in this cycle of violence (whether you're the batterer, victim, or the kid in the middle)--then I have some VERY specific messages that I feel that my God would stand behind me saying and adding his stamp of approval to that I must disclose to you.

TO THE BATTERER/OFFENDER: WHY do you try to seek your self-fulfillment in things that cannot satisfy? That hole in your heart is something that even your spouse should NEVER be expected to fill!! YOU CAN'T fill that hole with any material things, chemical substances, or even adrenaline rushes from letting off your anger! NOTHING else can satisfy like my GOD can!!!!!!!! I know it's hard to trust someone who wants to be your LOVING Father in Heaven above when you can't even conceive what a REAL man and father is like. But instead of trying to uselessly fill up that hollow hole in your soul and spirit with things that can't satisfy, why don't YOU put the loving Father and Creator of the Universe as YOUR spiritual center? Oh, WHY can't you try Him, test Him, taste and see that the Lord is good? He longs to love you, cradle you, shelter you in his loving arms, and be all of those things for you that the louse who was your earthly Father could never be for you? This Father that I know did the ultimate thing for you by allowing His ONLY Son die for you so that you can have a PERSONAL relationship with the ULTIMATE "Abba"/Father and so that king-sized hole in your heart can be filled once and for all. No Cinderella can ever fill those holes of loneliness, inadequacy, etc. like the God that I serve can!

TO THE VICTIM: Hey, Cinderella--why are you placing all of your hopes in that prince you're hoping will come someday? Or why are you trying to please a man that can never seem to be pleased? Prince Charming has NOTHING on a certain rich JEWISH bridegroom that I know--in fact, Prince Charming's a pauper next to the very King of Kings and Lord of Lords of the Universe. Even that Prince Charming's got to someday bow to Him, too!

Think about this for a moment--the Jewish people in ancient times had an interesting custom in regards to their wedding ceremony and celebrations. For one thing, whenever the groom was asked when he was going to be married, he would usually reply, "No man but my father knows the day or the hour." The groom would spend lots of time getting the wedding chamber just right until his father told him that it was time to go get his bride.

The bride, in the meantime, didn't have as much of a clue as the groom did of when the groom would come to take her away from her home. Therefore, she had to be in a state of constant readiness--knowing that her future husband might be there at any time to come take her away.

Ladies, do you want a real, wholesome FAIRY TALE that will come true? Then say "YES!" with all abandon to the Savior, Jesus Christ/Y'shua Ha'Meshiach, whose Father owns the cattle on a thousand hills! You want a REAL man with power, prestige, fame, and fortune? Then why don't YOU become a part of the Bride of Christ who will marry the richest Jewish bridegroom that the world has ever known? There is NO HIGH LIKE THE MOST HIGH GOD!! PRAISE HIS HOLY NAME!!

TO THE CHILDREN WHO ARE HURT BY THIS MONSTER MOST OF ALL: The loving Heavenly Father that I know DOES NOT DESIRE to beat you up or do something horrible to you!! He said to the prophet Jeremiah, "'For I know the plans I have for you,' declares the LORD, 'plans to prosper you and not to harm you, plans to give you hope and a future. Then you will call upon me and come and pray to me, and I will listen to you. You will seek me and find me when you seek me with all your heart.'" (Jer. 29:11-13, NIV) This loving Father desires also to keep you close to Him, protect you, and guide you in every step you take. DON'T let ANYONE take the future that my God and yours has given to you. Cling to it as best as you can--for it really is your life and hope!!

BUT THE BIGGEST MESSAGE OF ALL THAT I WISH TO GIVE ON THIS SUBJECT:

TO THE BODY OF CHRIST--We have sat here long enough and let Rome burn. We spend our time in our churches talking about massive building projects and the need to evangelize--when we will not even have the courage or willingness to serve those affected by this scourge of domestic violence. We talk about saving souls--but condemn those victims for things that are totally beyond control and are afraid to put the blame and responsibility on the head where it truly lies. If we would get our derrieres off our pews and into the domestic violence shelters and rescue those that are perishing a little more often, we might not have to worry as much about declining attendance in our churches. WE CANNOT expect them to come to us--FOR WE MUST FIRST COME TO THEM AND BEG AND PLEAD FOR THEM TO

COME TO HIM WHERE THEY ARE RIGHT NOW!! It's time to declare today as Independence Day for both Cinderella and Prince Charming--and do our part in helping to set both of them free through the power of His love!!!

[HOMEWORK;] Take some time this next week and do some DETAILED study NOT ONLY on the DISCUSSION QUESTIONS included with this lesson--BUT ESPECIALLY on the Scripture References that follow that directly relate to this lesson:
Eph. 4:17 through ch. 6:4 & ch. 6:10-18
James 1:2-27
Exodus 34:6
Ps. 30:5
1st Cor. 7:
Eccl. 9:9
Prov. 15:1 AND 29:11, 22-25
Gal. 5:13-26
1 Cor. 13:
AND DETAILED STUDIES ON THE FOLLOWING BOOKS:
******THE SONG OF SOLOMON (in regards to God's TRUE view of marriage)
HOSEA [God's view of us in sin in relation to marriage; how God desires us to treat a woman IN SPITE of the circumstances surrounding her]
1st JOHN (God's overall view of what love really is)

PRAYER: Creator Father, Lord God Almighty, and Lord Jesus/Y'shua:

Thank you today that you have allowed me to break free from the chains of the monster of domestic violence and to declare that from this day on that every day is now Independence Day for this (Cinderella/Prince Charming). Help keep me free from those chains that once bound me and help me keep in check those things that would bring me back to that bondage that I do not desire to be in ever again. Let your love flow through me, fill those empty places in my heart, and assure me through your loving care that you are truly MY loving Father who WILL NOT harm me--but who cares enough to take care of both the smallest and the largest needs that I have. I ask this today in Your Son's Name--AMEN!!

UNIT II, LESSON 4: A Jewel In His Crown--The Effects of
Childhood Sexual Abuse On All Of Us

At this juncture midway through this book, we have taken extensive time so far to go in-depth into the issues of sexual assault and domestic violence in a manner that lines up with God's Word has to say about these issues--and not man. But, as I have alluded to earlier in this book, my past experiences as a Grand Juror and also in prison ministry have led me to one conclusion--that if we are to ACTIVELY work to reduce the rate of recidivism in this country, if we ever expect to make a dent in the crime rate AT ALL, then it is absolutely vital that we in the Body of Christ get a grip and handle on two essential root causes: sexual assault and domestic violence.

But we wonder where all of this comes from to start with. I think it's time to roll out some vital evidence that expose our real enemy for who it/he/she is: gross violations of sexual abuse committed against our children--sometime even by those who are the closest to us (even, bleep forbid, done by those in the very name of our God and Creator Himself--despite the very fact that an act like this is totally abominable, detestible, and absolutely blasphemous to Him).

Now I AM NOT saying that I attribute the main reason for every major crime committed in this country to childhood sexual abuse--PLEASE DO NOT INTERPRET the things that follow in that way! But personally I have seen too much in various areas of our criminal justice system to make me wonder otherwise if somewhere in the backgrounds of a number of people who are currently incarcerated or in women who are victims of abusive husbands, etc. if somehow, some way that person may have been sexually molested in some fashion in their childhood. Notorious serial killers such as Ted Bundy and Henry Lee Lucas--I wonder if someone in the past robbed them of their childhood by an atrocious act like this. No wonder some men and women could be so willing to sink to such abysmismal depths and actions! When the foundation is built on sand and/or is faulty to start with, is there any other possible result that one could imagine for such an unfortunate individual? (Matt. 7:24-27)

One book I have in my own personal book collection is written by therapist Beverly Engel. In it, she details her personal story of how first seventeen-year-old neighbor boy had shamefully introduced Beverly and a boy playmate to adult sexual behavior before she was intellectually or emotionally equipped to handle it. Engel also described the sexual molestation she went through by the husband of her mother's best friend--too hideous to even go into detail here in this setting--and her mother's unwillingness and inability to protect her from such abuse.

Engel describes the trauma and aftereffects of such an event in her book "The Right To Innocence": "As a result, I, too, suffered from many of the long-term effects of childhood sexual abuse. I had both a fascination with and hatred toward men. Like many victims, I became sexually promiscuous, using men for sex and allowing them to use me. Unable to trust them, I was so afraid they would hurt or abandon me that I hurt them first. However, despite my heightened sexual activity, I did not have orgasms. And from the the age of nine, when Steve's [the husband of Engel's mother's best friend] abuse began, I entered into a continuing battle to manage my weight. Initially, gaining weight was a way to make myself less attractive to men and thus protection from further abuse. Those extra pounds also acted as a cushion and buffer from the tremendous pain I had sustained as a child. I began to drink when I was in high school to escape my problems and to find the exhilaration and power I could get no other way. I was unable to maintain a long-term relationship, choosing partners who were unavailable, married, or unable to commit, or who were as damaged, immature, and incapable of intimacy as I.

"...I excelled academically and professionally. But as with other sexually abused victims, excelling in these areas was also a way of compensating for and coping with the sexual abuse. I "lost myself" in schoolwork, and later on by helping others as a therapist. It turned out to be chillingly similar to my compulsion to "lose myself" in alcohol. Many childhood sexual abuse victims go to extremes and lose themselves in serving others as a way of avoiding their pain. It is no coincidence that they often become doctors, nurses, teachers, social workers, and psychotherapists, helpers, caretakers, and often "rescuers". ("The Right To Innocence: Healing The Trauma of Childhood Sexual Abuse"; Beverly Engel, M.F.C.C. [with foreword by Eleanor Hamilton, Ph.D.); 1989; Random House, Inc. [New York]; pg. 10.]

But Engel isn't the only one who has suffered from such childhood trauma. Rebekah Johnston, director of women's ministry at Seattle's Metanoia Ministries, detailed her childhood experiences with incest in this manner: "Years ago I saw a card that reminded me of the emotional secrets I hid behind a well-constructed mask while I was growing up. It pictured a little girl, with golden braids in a pretty pink dress, hanging up laundry on a clothesline. Once I was that innocent little girl, happy to be a "mommy" to my younger brother, a nurse to my dolls, and a little helper to my mother.

"...Then a chain of events occurred that changed the course of my life. At age three, I learned from my aunt that I had an older sister who died at birth. "She was so beautiful," my aunt told me. "She was just perfect."

"...I asked my aunt many questions and became obsessed with this sister that I never knew. As I grew older, I knew secretly that I could never attain the same perfection that this little girl would have attained if she had lived.

"...My younger brother also shaped my poor self-image. Everything seemed to come so easily to him. I always tried to be just like him, but failed continually.

"...When I was eight years old, my family was involved in a serious car accident. My brother and I were separated from our parents for three months. This separation created a great sense of loss and abandonment in my life.

"...Then came the most devastating event of all: my grandfather molested me when I was nine. After the incest, my childhood slipped away like a thief in the night. My dolls were traded for a baseball and bat. When I played house with my girlfriends, I was always the husband. I was labeled a "tomboy" by others and secretly wished that I could be a boy.

"...I became my mother's protector, admiring and idolizing her. We became emotionally enmeshed as I became her confidante, her caretaker, and her surrogate husband. I withdrew emotionally and physically from my father who found refuge in his work to avoid emotional involvement or conflict related to the incest by my grandfather. I began to believe that emotional support and security could only be found in another woman.""

Johnston also further chronicles how this incident would eventually effect a 13-year marriage with a former husband and pushing her towards lesbianism, drug abuse, more domestic violence, and even suicide. (Article by Rebekah Baeder-Johnston, (C) 2000, published in April 2000 edition of "Exodus International North American Update").

But what does this most hideous of monsters of sexual assault--childhood sexual abuse and incest--truly look like? Octavia Carlos offers these insights in an article she wrote several years ago in regards to incidents of incest occurring within the African-American community:

(1.) Incest is ANY sexual activity between family members outside of a marital relationship. [(Ex.) Mother, father, children, stepparents, stepchildren, half-brothers and sisters, etc.]

(2.) Sexual activity may be defined as any touching of the body for sexual gratification. [(Ex.) fondling, intercourse, race, sodomy, lewd and confusing sexual comments, voyeurism, etc.]

(3.) [Characteristics of Victims of Childhood Sexual Abuse;]
(a.) Suffer intense emotional pain while attempting to hold on to secrets
(b.) Full of rage that is either outwardly expressed or internalized
(c.) Confusion over role reversals
(d.) False guilt and shame
(e.) Anger at adults who don't put a stop to the abuse
(f.) Feelings of helplessness
(g.) Problems with success, dissatisfaction, and attitude towards personal achievement and accomplishment
(h.) Constant search for validation by others
(i.) Problems with personal self-worth and value
(j.) Demonstration of extremes in personal sexual behavior (either promiscuousness or celibacy)
(k.) Withdrawal and depression

Ms. Curtis has this to add about the most important reason why incest tends to happen: "...For ten years, I have worked with adult survivors of incest. During that time, I have found that incest knows no color distinction or gender preference. Incest happens across the board no matter who you are. When friends and co-workers ask me gingerly, "You don't find incest happening much in black families, do you?", my answer is "Yes." The question disturbs me because it reflects the societal denial of incest, just like the denial of abuse in the family. Denial is the ingredient which allows the abuse to continue. I would submit that denial is commonplace in this situation because the assault of an innocent, trusting, and helpless child is considered to be such a heinous crime, and people do not want to believe that such a thing could happen.

"...Perpetrators abuse children by seducing them slowly. Incest and the onset of abuse is a well-thought out plan and is initiated in many ways. Here are a few common examples: Creating a special relationship with the child, asking them to keep benign secrets or bribing them with money, candy or special trips, tricking or lying to the child; or assaulting the child physically, then daring them to tell. After the abuse, the victim keeps it secret, protecting himself, the perpetrator, and the rest of the family. The abuser helps the abused to maintain the secret through blackmail. Blackmail includes tactics like threatening to "tell on them" and make it "their fault" (children already believe it is their fault, as adults are viewed as powerful people and are to be believed); or threatening to hurt a family member or a pet if the abused tells the secret. The abuser obviously has only his or her interest in mind. And, yes, females are also guilty of incest.

"...On the topic of denial, as mentioned earlier, family members or outsiders may notice a difference in [the] behavior of a child but may choose to ignore it. Be aware that in order for abuse to become a pattern--i.e., occur more than once--there must be collusion, albeit subconscious. As the child continues to keep the abuse secret, mood and behavior changes are ignored by family members, possible suspicions are quickly tossed out and excuses are made for the abuser's behavior, providing an environment for the abuse to continue." (taken from an article written by Octavia Carlos, "INCEST Happens in Black Families: What It Looks Like and What Should"; Everybody's: The Caribbean-American Magazine; November 30, 1995; pp. PG; taken from Ethnic NewsWatch (C) Softline Information, Stamford, CT; (C) 1999 Infonautics Corporation.)

Now that we have somehow established in a manner lining up with the Law of Moses about "...a matter must be established by the testimony of two or three witnesses" (Deut. 19:15), it's time that we bring forth to the stand the most important and most credible Witness of all--the Lord God Almighty Himself. We have the evidence before us of the damage that childhood sexual abuse has caused for all of us. But what might God say in His Word about all of this? What are His views on the subject? Let's use your DISCUSSION QUESTIONS this session to find out!

[DISCUSSION QUESTIONS;]
(1.) What was God's ORIGINAL idea about marriage and sex? What did He think about it? (Gen. 2:18-25)

_____

_____

(2.) Was incest and childhood sexual assault an original part of God's design? (Leviticus ch. 18: AND ch. 20:11-24)

_____

_____

(3.) Earlier in the book, we alluded to 2 Sam. 15: . To review again and refresh our memories, what was the synopsis of what happened here? And what were the final results and consequences of it?

_____

_____

(4.) On the basis of the above, does God condemn this and any other type of sexual behavior on the part of the perpetrator? How does God view those who participate in such practices? (1 Thess. 4:4 & 5; 1 Cor. 6:13; 1 Pet. 4:2 & 3; Col. 3:5; Jude 4; Rom. 13:13; 1 Cor. 6:9; 2 Cor. 12:21; Mark 7:21; Gal. 5:19; Matt. 5: 27 & 28; Prov. 6:27; 1 Cor. 7:5)

_____

_____

(5.) BUT--to the victims to whom this crime was perpetrated against, what does God VERY MUCH wish to remind you about? What does He truly want you to know most of all? (Ps. 86:5; John 3:16; Rom. 5:8; Ps. 33:5; Jer. 31:3: 1 John 4: 8, 16, AND 19; 2 Cor. 13:11; 1 Chron. 16:34; Ps. 106:1; Eph. 2: 4 & 5; Ps. 25: 6 & 7; Rom. 8:38 & 39; 2 Cor. 1:3; Deut. 4:31; Ps. 116:5; Dan. 9:9; Lam. 3:22-24)

_____

_____

(6.) How does God regard Himself? How does He truly desire to relate to you? (1 Cor. 8:6; Ps. 68:5; 2 Cor. 1:3; Heb. 4:16 10:19, AND 12:15; Ps. 145;18; Jam. 4:8; Deut. 4:7; Ps. 145:19; 2 Cor. 9:8; 1 Cor. 1:4; Eph. 4:7; 1 Pet. 5:10; 1 Cor. 15:10; 2 Cor. 12:9; Isa. 54:8; Jer. 9:24 AND 31:3; Rom. 2:4; Acts 14:17)

_____

_____

I just heard an interesting song as I write this off of Steven Curtis Chapman's "Speechless" album called "Fingerprints of God" that I think sums up God's true opinion of you--NO MATTER what you have gone through or how you view yourself. Check this out real quick and see if this provides a lift of encouragement and a peace that God and His Son are still there without a shadow of a doubt in whatever storms you face:

"(1.) I can see the tears filling your eyes
And I know where they're coming from
They're coming from a heart that's broken in two
By what you don't see
The person in the mirror
Doesn't look like the magazine
Oh, but when I look at you it's clear to me...

[Chorus:] That I can see the fingerprints of God
        When I look at you
        I can see the fingerprints of God
        And I know it's true
        You're a masterpiece
        That all creation quietly applauds
        And you're covered with the fingerprints of God.

(2.) Never has there been and never again
Will there be another you
Fashioned by God's hand
And perfectly planned
To be just who you are
And what He's been creating
Since the first beat of your heart
Is a living, breathing, priceless work of art.

[Bridge:] Just look at you
        You're a wonder in the making
        Oh, and God's not through, no
        In fact, He's just getting started..."

To the victims who have experienced the trauma of childhood sexual abuse, incest, etc.--I really want to say this to you: Contrary to what you may think, God DOES CARE about you and LOVE YOU VERY MUCH! He absolutely GRIEVES with you to see what has been done to you and longs to hold you and embrace you in His loving arms as the father, mother, or whoever hurt you should have been. He desires to fix what is wrong with you and make it right if you will give Him the broken pieces of your life and allow Him and His Son to work His stuff and magic on you. NO--it WILL NOT happen overnight by any means--but He does promise that true recovery will come your way if you will wait patiently on Him and trust and rely on Him for all of your being.

YES--it is hard--VERY hard to trust in a loving Father God and Elder Brother Jesus/Y'shua when it seems all of the world of all sexes are totally against you. But after all that has been done to you, the fact remains that THEY STILL have not abandoned you completely. In fact, they're waiting on you right now to cry out to them and ask Them for Their most gracious help. No, DON'T think that you're weak because you're forced to call on Them--for They are YOUR LIFE! It is ONLY those who try to muddle through and think they can handle things themselves by putting on masks so that the world can't ever see who they truly are that never recover. They may think they can find recovery--but to me, it is only at best a mere putting up and coping with the problem. What seems better to you--merely taking your medicine and putting up with something the rest of your life...OR complete deliverance from what hinders you? I don't know what you might want--but I'd definitely rather like to take a taste of that deliverance stuff any old day!

Engel in the later part of her book recommends that those having gone through the trauma of childhood sexual abuse take the following process of recovery in what she terms "self-care":

Putting your own needs first
Valuing and respecting yourself
Praising and nurturing yourself
Asking for what you want and saying no to what you don't want

Recognizing that you have choices and rights
Having privacy and time alone
Doing only what you want with your body
Expressing your feelings, opinions, and needs
Making your own decisions
Trusting yourself
Learning to ask for what you want
Don't expect others to take care of you
Learn to say "NO!"
Value yourself
(Engel, pp. 189-201)

I personally believe that the above mentioned things that Engel says might have a little bit of value in someone's recovery--but I honestly don't feel that it goes far enough. WHY? Because it leaves out one vital and crucial step--GOD!! If God is not DEEPLY and INTIMATELY involved in your recovery, then nothing will ever truly be healed in your life. Solutions that do not take into account the crucial variable of God's infinite love, mercy, grace, care, and desires into the matter will NEVER go far enough.

To those who mock and say that God cannot be a viable solution to these problems, I'd like to fight back by giving you SEVERAL passages from the Psalms--written by a man who was a victim of MANY circumstances. YET--it did not phase him. In fact, he took some lickings and yet kept on ticking. Ps. 42:11 says, "Why are you downcast, O my soul? Why so disturbed within me? Put your hope in God, for I will yet praise Him, my Savior and my God." 3:3 also says, "But you are a shield around me, O LORD; you bestow glory on me and lift up my head." 46:1 says that "God is our refuge and strength, an ever-present help in trouble."

And for those who still aren't convinced, see what David wrote in the 91st Psalm:

"He who dwells in the shelter of the Most High will rest in the shadow of the Almighty. I will say of the LORD, "He is my refuge and my fortress, my God, whom I trust...Surely he will save you from the fowler's snare and from the deadly pestilence. He will cover you with his feathers, and under his wings you will find refuge; his faithfulness will be your shield and rampart. You will not fear the terror of night, nor the arrow that flies by day, nor the pestilence that talks in the darkness, nor the plague that destroys at midday. A thousand may fall at your side, ten thousand at your right hand, but it will not come near you. You will only observe with your eyes and see the punishment of the wicked. If you make the Most High your dwelling--even the LORD, who is my refuge--then no harm will befall you, no disaster will come near your tent. For he will command his angels concerning you to guard you in all your ways; they will lift you up in their hands, so that you will not strike your foot against a stone. You will tread upon the lion and the cobra; you will trample the great lion and the serpent. "Because he love me," says the LORD, "I will rescue him; I will protect him, for he acknowledges My name. He will call upon me, and I will answer him; I will be with him in trouble, I will deliver him and honor him. With long life will I satisfy him and show him my salvation."

To those who seek refuge and safety from your trauma and aftermath from incest and childhood sexual abuse, place your hope in the Most High God and Abba Father who wants to take you under His wing to the safest place that you will ever find yourself-- in His arms, His will, and His way. Let Him be your Comforter, Protector, Guide, and Shield. And in His due time and season, in Him you SHALL overcome. Note that I do NOT say MIGHT--I do not even say POSSIBLY--BUT SHALL OVERCOME! BARUCH HASHEM AND HALLELUJAH!!!! PRAISE HIS HOLY NAME THROUGHOUT ALL THE EARTH!!!!!!!!!

HOMEWORK: Take some time the next week to MEMORIZE as much as you can of Psalm 91: . Then, when the Adversary tries to remind you of who you once were and tries to tell you how unworthy you are, blah, blah, blah--HIT HIM BACK WITH THIS SCRIPTURE! Tell him you are a priceless and treasured kid of the King of Kings that dwells under His shelter and His love! (And then, if the Adversary tries to remind you of your past, YOU REMIND HIM OF HIS FUTURE! (Something, I think, involving a lake of burning fire--at least something like that!) So that way, if satan tries to attack, steal, kill, and/or destroy you, you can protect yourself spiritually by HITTING HIM with the Word of God. Then the Adversary will have NO choice but to flee and obey you RIGHT THEN and will cower and wimper and wonder what happen to you. And you can rejoice and be EXCEEDINGLY GLAD in Him!

PRAYER: Creator Father, Lord God Almighty, and Lord Jesus/Y'shua--I confess to You today that I don't know how to love You or even to accept the immense amount of love you have for me. Somebody (name who that person was) took that ability from me when (he/she--specify the act perpetrated against you). Father, I now realize that you are not that person. Help me to see just how much of a REAL Father that you truly are and that You really do love me as Your special child. Embrace me all throughout my being with Your love--the type of love that only You are able to provide. Help me not to try to search for love, validation, or anything else I might crave or need from any other source--but instead supply everything that I need so that my recovery and my joy may truly be complete. Show me now how truly loving and kind You are and never let me go from Your shelter in the heights. And protect me from those things that hinder me and try to separate me from the depths of your love. But most of all, Father, I thank You that You REALLY do care for me, that You REALLY love me, and that You will NEVER, EVER let me down no matter what I might do, say, act, or whatever--and that I'm YOUR child forevermore NO MATTER WHAT and that NOTHING can ever separate or keep me away from Your love ever again. And all of this I ask and say in your Son's Name--AMEN!!

UNIT II, LESSON 5: The Heart of A Woman--God's TRUE VIEW of the Roles and Standing of Men, Women, and Children

As a Christian single man (or at least as of the original writing of this book), I naturally am interested in working towards the development of intimate friendships and relationships with those of the opposite sex. Recently in my current efforts to pursue this goal, I have started checking into and signing up for several online personal ad services. Someone once said that "...a good man is hard to find." Some may say the same about a good woman--but now I'm not exactly sure about the validity of such a statement after some of the exploratory journeys that I have made into this new area of experience for me. It has been, to say the least, a very thrilling ride.

I have been very surprised to see some of the women that seem to have some of the high caliber, standards, and quality that I seek in the lady that might become my future bride. And, man--I want some of them so bad I can taste it--UUMPH!! It's frustrating to find out what is available out there, but you can't exactly take advantage of some of those opportunities at the present time due to reasons that are beyond your control. [In fact, I found one last night who is--ooh, ooh, ooh-- delightful! "Walk to Emmaus", cowboy church, counselor in private practice, and a sexy blonde bombshell to boot--MAN, I want her BAD!!!!! BUT...I HATE IT when I can't even establish contact with her--it's frustrating indeed...In case you haven't noticed yet, even Christians like myself have what Joyce Meyer likes to call our "...fleshy moments". We also have our carnal and natural desires, too--our Savior just desires for us to keep them in reasonable check and control, that's all. But for now, at least, we're unfortunately human, too.

Oh--you're wondering what I've put in my ads so far? Well, it's usually been along the lines of this: "Single white Christian male in early 30s who prefers to keep certain Jewish traditions, but attempts to have a Godly spirit in doing so, seeks an EXTREMELY physically, intellectually, and spiritually attractive single White or Hispanic female 23-35 ..."...blah, blah, blah--no need to go too much further into this.. I think this gives enough of an idea on what some people would desire of someone of the opposite sex.

We ALL desire intimacy--in fact, we CRAVE it! (I know I certainly do-- otherwise, I wouldn't be spending so much time websurfing through the personal ads like I have been recently.) It's a natural desire and urge that our God has graciously and generously given to us to bond intimately and closely with someone of the opposite sex. He has, in fact, blessed and sanctified a LEGITIMATE union between a man and a woman through marriage so much that He personally has put both immeasurable blessings not granted to you in any other way as well as numerous prohibitions and hedges of protection around it to keep an unblemished, sanctified relationship appropriately established within the bonds of holy matrimony a special, unique, and highly cherished relationship that will last into eternity. I know I like the sound of that--do you?

One of the main problems, though, in anyone that has gone through a situation related to sexual assault or domestic violence is the fact that a precious understanding of what the TRUE roles of men, women, and children within a family is either distorted, destroyed, devastated, or lost entirely to these EVIL MONSTERS and barbarians that have sneaked into our gates unawares and caused immense division and havoc in our families. Children who are brutally and maliciously molested lose even this ability to identify with their own sex and/or be able to have healthy and appropriate relationships with the opposite sex. Children who are forced to live in an environment of domestic violence early in life unknowingly pick up wrong patterns of behavior that will impact how they might relate to their future spouse. Women who are victims of sexual assault lose even their sense of confidence in themselves, sense of safety and protection, and security in their surroundings, and their ability to confide intimately with someone of the other gender. And worst of all, the chances of someone also being affected by other addictions and personal problems increases greatly when domestic violence and/or sexual assault has been an element of their past:

***Alcoholism   ***Juvenile delinquency
***Drug abuse   ***Homosexuality/lesbianism
***Suicide   ***Increased chances of future medical
                problems

Let me ask you this--if someone tried to fondle you or touch you in a sexual manner in ways you did not wish to be touched, would it be vile and repulsive to you? Would you resist with all your strength and might that person's attempts to humiliate and degrade you? OF COURSE YOU WOULD!! No one in their right mind would dare tolerate such actions. But let me ask you this--after the incident took place, would you be likely to put your trust in that person for ANYTHING ever again? How willing would you be to forgive them for what they did to you and allow your relationship with them to be fully restored?

These questions can impact people for the rest of their lives and will not allow them to fully recover from the problems they have faced save for God's grace. It can even impact their views of how they see God as their Heavenly Father and their willingness to come under His umbrella of authority. And it can even prevent some people from obeying established authorities on this earth--governmental or otherwise. How can someone look up to a father figure when the best picture of a father they can conjure up in their mind is the man in their childhood who beat them and their mother or the one who violated them sexually at an early age and did heinous things to them that I dare not describe due to the sensitivities of others? No wonder we have such problems! When your views and conceptions of the proper roles of men and women are distorted to start with, then confusion and destruction reigns in our families and in our world.

Back in Lesson 3 of this unit, I referred to a story about the class of prisoners that I had the opportunity to assist someone else in teaching. Please allow me now to go a little more in detail about one of the lessons that I was directly involved in with this group. One night, we focused on the roles that men should have within the Church. I didn't know why at first, but I felt led of the Spirit to bring my chess set along with me into the unit. I wasn't even for certain if the chess set would even clear security or not--but praise God that it did...for I know that God had a purpose in my doing so. It seems that I like to talk and teach in the form of visual illustrations and roleplaying so that even male prisoners with absolutely little formal education could easily get a grasp of what I was talking about.

Anyway, as I begun my portion of the lesson, I had the small group of men two at a time that knew how to play chess (which happened to be most of them--which thrilled me a lot having played seriously in a few tournaments myself in the past). I allowed the first two to start the game, then after a few minutes I stopped them in the middle of their play and had the next two men continue the game right where it was-- and so on and so forth down the line.

In the process of this "controlled chaos", I also simultaneously had one of the inmates read some Scriptures dealing with roles and functions while the chess game was going on. After a little bit of time was taken with the chess activity, I then was led to bring the lesson to a close by challenging the men to also consider the roles that women and children can play in His work. To say the least, I was privileged to learn a little bit about what was in their hearts and minds and encourage the men to try to see things from other perspectives outside of themselves and get a better grasp of how God might view our unique roles and functions in His Son's Body.

I wonder, men, how you see yourselves in relation to His Body and also how you see the equal importance of the vital roles that women and children play within the

Church at large. And ladies--how do you see men in relation to your Father in Heaven? Do you see them as brutes that do nothing but hurt or victimize you--or as a deeply caring unselfish provider willing to do ANYTHING for you (even sacrifice his life for you if need be)? You see, if our views of the roles of each gender are distorted and do not line up with the Word of God, then satan already has us in his sights before we leave the starting gate.

The prophet Hosea said about Israel: "...my people are destroyed from lack of knowledge..." (Hosea 4:6) Let's not be ignorant of the necessary and vital part our God wants us to play in this drama and let's instead acknowledge how valuable God sees each one of us individually as well as others who work in His Body--AND on top of that, how EQUALLY precious WE ALL ARE in His sight. Let's take some time through our DISCUSSION QUESTIONS to go a bit more in-depth in discovering those things our God might desire for us to know about the unique places that He has set at His table for us and shed the "stinkin' thinking" and distortions that the Adversary has used to keep us chained and bound:

[DISCUSSION QUESTIONS:]

(1.) Let's first look at 1 Cor. 12: for a moment or two. What does the Rav Shaul/Apostle Paul say are the gifts of the Spirit? What are some of the unique things that God can manifest in each of us?

_____

_____

(2.) (v. 12-26) Now what does Paul wish to say to the Corinthians about what the Body of Christ is all about?

_____

_____

(3.) (v. 27-31) And what does Paul say about what the offices of the "fivefold ministry" is about?

_____

_____

[(Note:) I like what the Promise Keepers Bible has to say
about the latter part of 1 Cor. 12: --"...Paul liked to use
the human body as an illustration of the relationship
believers have with one another. As members of the body of
Christ, God lives in every believer; his presence links
believers together. Just as each cell in your body is attuned
to every other cell and receives direction from one brain, so
also in Christ's body (the Church) the Spirit establishes a
connection between each cell and the Head, and among all the
cells of his body, God has called you as a Christian to join
a body that binds you together with other diverse cells."

The PK Bible also goes on to say these important things
about the above:
   (1.) Your bond in the Spirit links you together with every
other Christian in the world. Without each committed
Christian, Christ's Body would be incomplete.
   (2.) Second, we must honor each other and each one's
unique contributions to the Body of Christ.
   (3.) We must care for each other--for if one hurts,
everyone else does, too!

(4.) But with our gifts, talents, abilities, and offices also
come some responsibilities and obligations that we must not
neglect. What does Paul admonish overseers and deacons to
avoid? And could these things apply to all of us today? (1
Tim. 3:1-12; Titus 1:5-3:11)

_____

_____

(5.) Now since a major part of our problems in the areas of
domestic violence and sexual assault involve misconceptions
and misunderstandings over how women are seen and treated,
we're now going to take some time to stop here first and park
a while so that God's Word can finally for once penetrate our
minds and help us get rid of thinking patterns that are not

like Him and His ways:

(a.) Let's zero in first on Prov. 31:10-31. This chapter in particular has a lot to say about what a REAL woman should be. What does this chapter say about what the "...virtuous woman" is like? Describe IN DETAIL some characteristics you see about this woman.

_____

_____

(b.) Now look closely in particular at verses 11 and 28. Do these verses say that her husband abuses or mistrusts her? Does her husband knock her down, slap, kick, or punch her? How does this husband treat this woman?

_____

_____

(c.) Look at verses 10 and then 28-36. How is this virtuous woman truly regarded by all?

_____

_____

[(Special Note:) In most Jewish homes, Prov. 31: is also read over the wife by the husband as an important part of the weekly Sabbath Seder AS A BLESSING over her! Talk about kindling a romantic fire...]

(6.) But there are other verses in Proverbs that describe how a husband should view his wife. What does Prov. 12:4 and 18:22 say about a wife? (Also--how about 1 Tim. 3:11?)

_____

_____

(7.) And Paul has something else to say to you about who you are in Christ. What exactly does he say? (Gal. 3:26-4:7; EMPHASIS on 3:28!)

_____

_____

(8.) But you don't have to have a husband or boyfriend to be special to God. Who were some women that God has used throughout Scripture as examples of leadership? [Ex. 15:20; Judges 4:4" 2 Kings 22:1-20; 2 Chron. 22:10-23:21; Acts 16:11-15; 18:1-4 AND 18-26; Rom. 16:]

_____

_____

(9.) But in the midst of all this, everything that we all do must also be accompanied and tempered with the fact that we should already be displaying those virtues and character traits that God says will lead to prosperity and good success in these areas if we will diligently seek, obtain, and apply them.

(a.) What does God's Word require of a wife? (1 Pet. 3:1; 1 Cor. 7:10 AND 11:3; Eph. 5:22 AND 33; Col. 3:18)

_____

_____

[Note my glorified opinion on this subject...When the Word says or mentions the word "submit" (I know that these days it can be a dirty word for some, but I prefer to go by what the Word says, NOT man.), it does NOT imply that you have to be limp-wristed milktoast for an abusive husband and take his abuse. In situations like this, GOD is then the one you must follow and you need to follow HIS wisdom and guidance on what to do. But the idea of submission in the Bible is this--if a husband is NOT otherwise severely out of line with His ways, then it is absolutely necessary for you ladies to allow that husband to make the decisions that he feels are for the benefit and welfare of your family and that you stand behind and support.

AND even if your husband is a complete imbecile and worthless twit of a creature, the words of 1 Pet. 3:1-6 come into play. Now obviously this MUST be done with His wisdom guiding your way. There's a point where even common sense and self-protection has to take precedence. But for you ladies that have trouble with this submission thing, it's fortunate that I can maybe give you a perspective based on male machismo to help you grasp this better.

Do you know why we men might tend to not listen as much to you when you talk to us in ways that WE men might perceive in our eyes as nagging, bellyaching, and complaining? From a man's perspective, I'll give you ladies a dirty little secret you might not know about. It's because those men who are out there in the work world face this exact thing from our employers and others. We men tend to have pretty focused attention on only those things that are important. We can't necessarily go out and deal with ten thousand things at once like you ladies can. Men deal with the big things and major goals and challenges while ladies in general tend to be much more detail-oriented and capable of handling the little things. When you ladies bombard us men with requests of ANY kind that are currently out of our frame of reference and personal interest too soon before we've had a proper chance to transition from what we were dealing with to what you're asking, it tends to be a little too much for us.

We men don't like to feel harassed, nagged, and pushed (or. at least, what we may THINK in our view as being such). INSTEAD, we feel better and more comfortable with you and are more willing to try to accommodate what you wish if we as men feel like you ladies respect, honor, cherish, and (bleep forbid that I must use this term) OBEY us. Men the biggest part of the time have to deal with a siege mentality--we'd
like to have at least one place of personal refuge where we don't have to fight, scratch, and claw for what we want in life (and yes, if need be--SLEEP!). Men like their homes to be castles in which their wives respect them and stand behind and support what they do no matter what the outside world says to them otherwise. Usually, if you ladies will keep this in mind in dealing and putting up with us men, you might find the relationships with your husbands (or, as the case might be, your future spouse, if any) down the road to be easier to handle and much more enjoyable for
the two of you.]

(b.) But to our male counterparts, you aren't getting off
completely scot-free, neither. There's things that God
expects you to do, too. What does His Word say they are?
(1 Cor. 7:3-5; 1 Pet. 3:7; Eccl. 9:9; Col. 3:19; Prov. 5:15
AND 18; 1 Tim. 5:8; Eph. 5:22-28 AND 33; Gen. 2:24)

[Sidebar Note: I forget exactly where I heard this from, but I think that the following observation does make a lot of sense. I remember someone (I think it was Duane Sheriff--but don't take my word on that) saying something along the lines of this in a sermon one time that the reason why God seems to tell husbands to love their wives while telling the wives to obey and respect their husbands is this--He seems to explicitly encourage and command each gender to do things that are totally the opposite of what their normal human natures would otherwise dictate. For instance, women are naturally motivated by relationships based on unconditional love and acceptance of a person and are usually not hesitant to show and communicate that love to others. Men, on the other hand, tend to develop relationships based on trust, past performance and reliability, and mutual admiration. For example, think of the types of toys each gender plays with during childhood. Girls tend to play dolls and have tea parties while the boys might generally engage in more physical activities and roughhousing with one another.

In a marriage relationship, though, the man and woman tend to come from diametrically opposite sides of the track as far as their modus operandi of establishing and maintaining relationships goes. Men like myself tend to find it hard to express and communicate love while women have a difficult time dealing with criticism and submission to authority because of concerns of whether or not they might be liked, accepted, and valued as a person. That's why it seems God felt it necessary to devote valuable portions of Scripture to encourage men to show affection to their wives and wives to GRACIOUSLY and LOVINGLY WITHOUT COMPLAINT get behind, uphold, and support the authority of their husbands and not do anything inappropriate to sabotage the leadership of their spouse.

The reason why? It's BECAUSE the performance of these commands will more fully satisfy the deepest longings and cravings of the other person more than anything else you can do for the spouse. When a man shows and demonstrates outward affection towards his wife, then the wife feels validated and valued by her spouse. When a woman obeys and respects her man and supports him in his personal efforts, the man's deepest longings for respect are then quenched and he feels much more confident and protected enough to allow his weaknesses and vulnerabilities show to his spouse without feeling like he has to walk through an emotional minefield to get to some sort of place of safety and comfort.]

(10.) Now let's talk about the kids for a minute, too, while we're on the subject on the discussion of God-ordained roles in the family.

(a.) How does God view children in general? How did even our Savior regard them--and what did He say about them? (Prov. 23:24; Ps. 127:3; Col. 3:20; Luke 18:16; Prov. 17:6: Matt. 19:14; Mark 10:13-16) (b.) What, though, are children obligated by God to do for their parents? (Ex. 20:12; Deut. 5:16; Matt. 15:4 AND 19:19; Mark 10:19: Luke 18:20; Prov. 1:8, 6:20, AND 23:22; Eph. 6:1; Col. 3:20; Lev. 19:3)

The heart of the matter to all is this--If each of us men and women could understand what is in each other's hearts and what would satisfy the other's deepest emotional cravings, maybe the percentage of incidents of domestic violence and sexual assault would dwindle. When we each can cherish and value someone's unique role and part in the Body of Christ and in our relationship to them and the special contributions that each one can make to the whole, there will then be less incentive for strife and more incentive for cooperation, harmony, and love. And, most of all, when God is allowed to be the Ultimate Ruler, Authority, and Judge over the whole family, peace can reign and destruction and heartache can be a distant memory in the rear view mirror. And when we begin to understand and listen to the TRUE heart of a woman, happiness and joy can flood our families instead of anger, grief, sorrow, and pain.

Speaking of women...hmmmm....seems like I just got an e-mail back today--can't believe that I got a response to that ad already...WELL, who do we have here? Uh,,,LORI? hmmm...Well, howdy there, madam...I wonder if she's the one from San Angelo whose ad I saw that said that she worked in corrections and that if you couldn't keep a job to just please move on. (I wonder what she would think if she knew I had THREE part-time jobs I'm holding on to right now. I'm responsible, I think...It's just the simple fact that I'm broke right now--that's all...Hmmm...says that yes, she would like to talk with me some more--and where am I from?..."Well, I'm a high straight in Plainview..." Looks like she has a Web page to go to here-- FloraCora? I wonder why in the bleep she has that as part of her e-mail address...ah, well, I guess
that'll be the fun part of it all--the mystery, let it unravel gradually...And it looks like her Web page is about a horse farm in Big Lake...Too bad I'm allergic to cats, dogs, and possibly horses....A Mister Patchity Patch is available for stud...15 1/2 hands, very broad in chest and rear...Such a shame I don't know diddly-squat about horses....Interesting horse, though..."A horse is a horse, of course, of course..."

[HOMEWORK: It's role reversal time again here! Take some time out real quick to roleplay how you might normally handle a situation of conflict involving your spouse. (Ex.--A request for them to mow the lawn) Then, think a little bit, in light of the information you have learned in this lesson, about how your spouse might react to that request from THEIR perspective. Then switch sides in that roleplaying situation and act out their part and see what happens.)

[PRAYER:] Creator Father, Lord God Almighty, and Lord Jesus/Y'shua: Thank you for enlightening me today about how You view each of us not only in Your Body, but also in our families. Thank You for teaching me just how much You value and care for me and also what you would desire and expect from me. Help me keep this information in mind any time I deal with relationships of any kind or nature with the opposite sex and assist me in acting towards others in a manner that pleases and honors You in this area. And help me implement it so that I might have true peace and love in every relationship I pursue. I say this in Your Son's name and for His sake--AMEN!

UNIT III, LESSON I--COMING BACK HOME FROM VIETNAM

I remember quite well the day I came back home from my Vietnam. No, I was way too young to have even been able to go through the Vietnam War, much less fight in it. I wasn't hardly in kindergarten when the War ended. But I know a little bit of how it is to go through a war in your emotions that never seems to end.

Some people in certain theological circles may have severe criticism and intense questioning to those who deal with concepts such as spiritual warfare, demonic possession, and things of that nature. I know for certain that there was once a time where I surely either didn't know much about it at all or, worse, considered those who practiced such theological concepts to be full of the devil himself. But, after what happened to me one Memorial Day weekend, it will be very much harder for me personally to raise those same criticisms ever again. Whether or not this "spiritual warfare" thing has grounds with anything in Holy Scripture, I don't honestly know. I think I'll let the more scholarly theologians and nationally prominent religious figures battle that one out. But after what happened that weekend, I will only say one thing for sure--without a few people that I know who work in this particular area, I certainly feel that I would have never come back home from the Vietnam-like struggles of the past I once faced.

It was interesting how it all happened. I forget whether or not I had decided deliberately to stay home from my home church in another city that I would usually go to that weekend or if I had trouble getting a ride there. It just happened to be that one of the non-denominational churches in the city where I live was having a "deliverance weekend". I had been to this place a time or two before for similar things and also to the local "cowboy church" that this particular church hosted once a month. I originally didn't take much stock in this concept...UNTIL this particular Memorial Day weekend came.

This time proved to be so radically different for me than other times. It was as if a compulsion came over me to come to this weekend and behave in extremely unorthodox ways in my manner of worship to Him than I was personally accustomed to--just compelling me that I just had to be there, no matter what effort it took for me to get there.

It wasn't the fact that I had to walk over a mile one way to where the meeting was held--that to me didn't seem unusual. NO--it was the fact that during this weekend, I constantly felt compelled to do two things. One--that I had to make a COMPLETE list of ALL of the prayer concerns and needs that I wanted to pray over for myself and others. The second? (And this was REAL strange to me...) It was that during any of those times I might want to pray (especially during the ministry time), I could ONLY pray in one position--prostrate face down on the ground lying as if I were shooting a target with a rifle.

But why this thing about praying ONLY in a prostrate position? Part of it was the compulsion of what I felt I needed to do within the spirit of that particular moment I was in. But the other reason was even more Scriptural in nature. I found this out during a previous one-day fast that I went through in which I found myself not being able to pray to the Lord effectively in any other way EXCEPT to completely lie prostrate. A picture that was burned in my mind that I saw on a made-for-TV movie was very prevalent in my thinking at that time--a picture of King David himself going into total abandon in his worship and praying entirely in a prostrate position. But what got me really in this mood to pray prostrate was when I looked up the word "prostrate" in the concordance in my Bible. There are only two times that I could reasonably find that very word in Scripture--and both of those are located in Deut. 9 in the New International Version when Moses was making his final address to the Israelites. [Can you guess what BOTH of those instances within that chapter (verses 18 and 25, that is) refer to? The answer might surprise you. Look it up real quick as an exercise--and you'll see what I mean.]

Now back to the weekend. This went on through both of the services of that deliverance meeting that Sat. Then I had to get back to reality. I did some other things that night and went to bed, noting that I had to do laundry first thing in the morning. The next morning, I was again compelled by the Spirit to go back to that church--THIS TIME to schedule a personal appointment for ministry. One slight little problem with this, though...THE LAUNDRY!! And a BIGGER problem in doing the laundry? The laundry room in the apartment complex where I lived at that time operated on a time lock that closed the place between 8 PM until 8 AM. Believe me, when I got up at around 7 to 7:30 the next morning, it was a VERY long wait for the laundry room to open back up to get the laundry done.

By the time I was finally able to get into the place and get the laundry started, it was 8:30--and the church service at that place starts at 10:00. By the time I was finally able to get to that church, the folks were already most of the way into the music service. But nevertheless, I managed to slip a note to the pastor of that church requesting an appointment for that afternoon. After the service, I spoke with that pastor--and he said to speak to his wife and that she would set up a time for me. I did--and arrangements were made for later in the afternoon (which, by the time I left there for the lunch break so that I could finish folding the clothes that I wasn't able to do during my rush to get to the church service--it would prove to be an hour-and-a-half later).

When I came back for that appointment, needless to say--I came prepared. I had to first wait on the folks on the ministry team to handle those that were from out-of-town as a courtesy to them so that they could have time to get back to their homes at a decent hour. Then, my time came and both of the wives of the pastor and one of the assistant pastors would later prove to be the ones performing ministry on me.

When I came in the room, the very first thing I did was to spread out a number of things that I had put in a duffle bag as points of contact to pray over. Then guess what happened AGAIN? You got it--I wound up face down on the floor again. (For an EXTREMELY fat man like me, it's, to say the least, a VERY uncomfortable position to be in--ESPECIALLY in terms of being able to breathe properly!!] When they did their initial assessment of my situation, I told them all that I had been felt compelled to do throughout most of that weekend up to that point and the things that I had needs that I desired prayer for quite a number of issues.

I was quite amazed to hear the response of one of the ladies after relating my concerns to them: "I think that we can take care of this by simply dealing with the spirit of rejection." "All these needs could be taken care of by working with this?" I sarcastically thought to myself. "This surely can't be." Nevertheless, I went along with the flow of what the Holy Spirit seemed to want to do in that situation.

The first thing after that remark the ladies asked me to do was to sit up to where I could breathe. (That in itself was a relief--ESPECIALLY when I just couldn't do ANYTHING BUT pray in a prostrate position.) THEN--things got even more interesting from there. NO--in case you're wondering, I did not experience anything along the lines of "The Exorcist". (Besides, some things of a spiritual nature don't always necessarily require sound, fury, and thunder anyway. Some of our God's best little victories and most effective solutions are sometimes the most quiet ones of the Spirit.] INSTEAD--the ladies started speaking over me some of the most life-changing and affirming words I had ever heard. These were not as much "I rebuke you, Satan!" or things like you might commonly associate with flashy teleevangelists in today's media. They were for me more along the lines of "God loves Coy. God cares for Coy..." and so on and so forth.

But what eventually proved to the pinnacle of it all and the ultimate testimony of God's infinite insight, timing, and grace was when one of the men that was there who was trying not to intrude on what was happening actually would serve the most valuable role of all. I did not realize it until then--but it seemed that, above all else, there were some issues of father abandonment, rejection, and neglect that I had not worked through.up until that point. The very man who was trying not to intrude would actually be the very thing that gave what took place a whole lot more credibility. I will always remember what he said to me as I hugged this man for dear life as I for the first time in my life dealt with deeper issues that the previous problems I had went through so far in my life up to that point were at best mere symptoms of. This time, that root--the trunk of that tree, so to speak--was finally being destroyed for good as he said to me, "As a representative of Jesus Christ, I accept you as a man and affirm you for who you are." I may not have the exact words right and in their entirely--but the essence of the message that God gave to me through this man was this: "You've talked a lot about Vietnam and Siberia. Well, son, you are rejected no more. You can finally come back home from Vietnam."

I was literally crying a river of tears in the midst of this scene. Some people might call this unfoolish, unwise, and unsignified. But if that is the only way that my God felt that I could realistically come back from Vietnam, come back home from the rejection, the misery, the pain, the shackles of my emotional past, the devastation, and the loss of things I once held dear...then who am I to call the process that He may desire to liberate me from those things that hold me back as useless and stupid? How could I even think or dare to call the King of the Universe on the carpet for a method that isn't necessarily easy to fit in a certain box that I might otherwise imagine for Him?

After the ministry time was completed, I had occasion to ask one of the ladies (ESPECIALLY since I was still a little new to the concept of spiritual warfare) how she was able to tell and discern that the root problem of it all was that of rejection. She basically told me that it was by "observation and discernment of the Spirit" and that she could tell by the look on my face and in the way I acted when I was in the room and had literally surrounded myself with objects on the floor.

After I came back home from the church, I reflected a little bit on what had happened and then turned on the radio to a prominent Christian radio network. The song that I heard not too long after I turned on the radio gave even more of a bit of closure and the turning of all the events to a completed full circle. It was a special honoring veterans for Memorial Day that I happened to come upon that had a song by Ray Boltz called "It's An Honor To Serve" that I will also remember for a long time to come. As I sang the chorus of that song, I could hardly keep from thinking one thing: The wars that I have faced are finally over now--and I have as of now OFFICIALLY in my mind and heart FINALLY come back home from my Vietnam.

Back home from the chains that had bound me--and back from the pain and grief that I had suffered through. And I couldn't help but especially sing this line with gusto: "It's an honor, an honor to serve." I was now officially dismissed by Him to move on to other things that life had to offer and dismissed from the duties and responsibilities of the past.

Some time later, I had occasion to assist another prison ministry at a prison unit in another town. As a part of this, all of the members that went to one of the units on the part of the crusade team that I was on prayed over the Chaplain of that unit as we felt was in harmony with the moving of the Holy Spirit. Somehow in this process during the second time we prayed over him after that service, I felt led to pray for this Chaplain that he be delivered from the spirit of rejection and did so appropriately. It turned out that I had previously heard a little bit about this man through the prison ministry grapevine about him in regards to possible problems at the time that he may possibly be having in regards to time management and organizational skills. During the course of this, this Chaplain had mentioned that he was a veteran of the Vietnam War. Somehow that came up in my prayer over him, too.

After we finished the crusade, the head of this ministry remarked that he thought that I might have the spiritual gift of discernment because he had previously discussed these issues with this Chaplain before--AND that I had seemed to pick up on this WITHOUT ANY prior knowledge whatsoever of that particular situation. This also amazed me in itself. But what was more remarkable on my end was my response to his remark: "...I don't call it discernment. I consider it only hard-earned experience at best since I have been myself previously delivered from that same spirit."

The experience I had at that "deliverance weekend" makes me wonder about the following: Could it be that a possible ROOT CAUSE of your turmoil in various areas of your life be attributed to possible spiritual effects of rejection, abandonment, etc. from one or both of your parents? Could the valid reason for your current troubles be partially be due to the fact that certain issues in your own life have NOT been completely, fully, and honestly dealt with in the way that they should be properly dealt with? Is your search for love, fulfillment, and favor in the eyes of man instead of God a possible cause for your current pain and heartache--and are these things also partially due to these issues? Let's go IMMEDIATELY into our DISCUSSION QUESTIONS section this time and find out for ourselves!!!

[DISCUSSION QUESTIONS:] (1.) What would YOU think that God
and HIS WORD says about YOU and these issues of rejection,
abandonment, etc.? WHAT DOES HE TRULY THINK OF YOU AS? How
does our Heavenly Father TRULY treat you and feel about you?
What are YOUR personal thoughts towards this?

(2.) How do WE usually perceive God? How might WE normally
think about what God is, who He is, and what He does? [Check
Lamentations 5: --WITH an emphasis on verses 19 through 22.]

(3.) But what does GOD SAY about all of this? [Read Heb. 6:9,
10, & 13-22; chap. 12: 22-29; and chap. 13:5b-8.]

(4.) What might the following passages have to do and/or say
about the subject of rejection as well as how one should
properly view his/her relationship with God? {Read Ps. 68:4-
6; Ps. 103: 13-18; Luke 11:11-13; Rom. 8:15-17; and 2 Cor.
1:3 & 4.]

Keener contributes here an interesting insight on the
above passage in Romans:

"...Here Paul again plays on the idea of the exodus from
Egypt; God's glory led his people forward, not back toward
slaver. (cf. Ex. 13:21; Zech. 2:5)...although only a few
Roman Jews spoke Aramaic, Jesus' special address for his
Father as "Papa" had become a name for God in early Christian
prayers (Gal. 4:6), perhaps by Jesus' design (Matt. 6:9).
Roman adoption--which could take place at any age--canceled
all previous debts and relationships, defining the new son
wholly in terms of his new relationship to his father, whose
heir he thus became...
"...Philosophers spoke of conscience testifying (cf. 2:15;
9:1); Jewish people believed that the Spirit had testified to
God's truth against Israel and the nations by the prophets.

But here the Spirit's prophetic message is good news to the believer's heart. As a legal act, Roman adoption (cf. 8:15) had to be attested by witnesses; the Spirit is here the attesting witness that God adopts believers in Jesus as his own children..." (Keener, pp. 429 & 430).

Something else in Keener's commentary, though, is interesting to note in regards to the beginning of Paul's 2nd Letter to the Corinthians:

"...It was customary in the ancient world to include a prayer or offering of thanks to a deity in letters of substantial length (as most of Paul's extant letters are). One of the most common forms of Jewish prayer was a benediction or praise that began, "Blessed [praised] be God, who..."; this was a way of glorifying God for his works. A regular "synagogue prayer" addressed God as the "merciful Father"...which is what "Father of mercies" (cf. "Father of compassion"--NIV) means...
"...God would bring his final comfort to his people with the Messiah's coming (e.g., Isa. 40:1; 49:13), but he also comforted them in their hardships during the present (e.g., Ps. 94:19) The principle that suffering teaches one how to treat others is rooted in the Old Testament (Ex. 23:9). Paul's specific comfort in this verse is that he found Titus well and with good news about the Corinthians (2 Cor. 7:4, 6 & 7, 13; cf. 2:2 & 3)..." [Keener, pg. 483]

I could give more...but if these things don't show you in a very definite way God's deep, abiding love for you--NOTHING EVER WILL!!! He HAS NOT rejected or abandoned you--but INSTEAD as our Savior Himself said in Matt. 28:20: "...And surely I am with you always, to the very end of the age." SO WHY DON'T YOU DIVE IN RIGHT NOW without hesitation to His ageless, limitless love!! GO ON, I SAY...WHAT'S STOPPING YOU????? WHAT HAVE YOU GOT TO LOSE??? COME ON--DON'T BE BASHFUL!! DIVE IN RIGHT NOW!!!

You see, the Adversary would LOVE for you to think of yourself as much less than you truly are!! But the Father and Son operation that is the Kingdom of God have something TOTALLY different about how much in high regard they think of you and how truly and highly esteemed that you are in Their eyes! 2 Cor. 5:17-21 literally proves it--WE ARE THE RIGHTEOUSNESS OF GOD THROUGH OUR MESHIACH/SAVIOR!! He paid the absolute highest price for someone like you NOT because you deserve it or that you did something to earn it--BUT IN SPITE of who you are!! You don't have to stand there believing the lies of our enemy! YOU CERTAINLY DON'T have to think of yourself as less than what God truly thinks of you! YOU ARE NO LESS THAN A CHILD OF THE KING!! SO BLEEP IT--DON'T BE AFRAID TO ACT LIKE IT!!

You ARE NOT rejected by Him--but, to the contrary, VERY HIGHLY loved, respected, and cared for by our loving Creator and Father of all. And His Word for you today is that you CAN come back home from the wars you've faced and the fierce battles that you have been forced to fight. And the best part of it all--when all of our work is through here and we stand before Him for our rewards in His kingdom, guess what He has in store for you!! For the ones who overcome, I wouldn't be surprised if He decides to throw a "Welcome Home" party of the likes that none of us has ever seen and a tickertape parade with the cheering crowds that you have waited so long to see.

Instead of coming home in disgrace and confusion, you will finally for once come back a hero with an air of confidence about you. Instead of protest marches and boos, you will hear the cheers, applause, and roars from the crowd in approval as YOUR name is announced. I'll tell you this much--watching a 4th of July parade will seem boring compared to this bash! And what will it all be in celebration for? It will be for the fact that you were finally able to come back home from your Vietnam.

And when you come home, don't be surprised if I myself might be up there in the stands cheering you on and smiling as your family runs up to you and hugs and kisses you wildly. Why? Because I know for myself what it's like to come back home from personal experience--and because a few people that I know personally helped bring me back home from my Vietnam, too!! I'll be celebrating with you, too, because I know one thing is true. Be it ever so humble--there's no place like home. Welcome back home, old friend--welcome back. You've been gone way too long--and we missed you while you were gone. The war is now OFFICIALLY over and the victory is won. Welcome back home, sailor--welcome home.

HOMEWORK: This next week, think of someone who may have rejected you--either in the past or even maybe recently. And also take some time to think about someone YOU may have rejected in some fashion yourself in one way or another. THEN--try to in both cases as best as you are able to REPLACE that rejection with love and acceptance and then see what happens as a result. Come back in the next session prepared to relate the results of this experiment to your fellow group members.

PRAYER: Creator Father, God Almighty, and Lord Jesus/Y'shua: Thank You for showing us today that You have NOT rejected us or cast us aside--but that instead that You love us with an everlasting love and that through all that we do that You still care for us IN SPITE of who we truly are. I praise You that there is still something about me that You will always love no matter what I might do or say. Help me to accept Your love and NEVER deny it or doubt it in ANY way. And help me more fully see how You truly view me through Your eyes and NOT the eyes of this world. Thanks for Your abundant grace and mercy that assures me that I am never too far from Your loving care and that I will always be Your child come what may. Help me to remember these things at those times when everyone else around me might reject me for one reason or another--that YOU STILL have not turned your back on me AND NEVER EVER WILL...not anytime right now in the present, not anytime soon, or even at anytime throughout the rest of eternity. And thank You most of all for letting me come back home from my Vietnam and come back home to You. In your Son's name I pray-AMEN!!!

UNIT III, LESSON 2--WALKING A MILE IN SOMEONE ELSE'S MOCCASINS

There is an old American Indian proverb that I feel puts what I am fixing to say here in perspective. It goes, "Don't judge someone until you have walked a mile in someone else's moccasins." During various times when I have been involved in prison ministry, I have seemed to notice that the slightest, foggiest notion that they need to be TRULY concerned about the needs of the victim AND to furthermore fulfill the letter and spirit of the above proverb hasn't even been brought forth in their minds. I also wonder if they had a slight clue about the experiences the victim goes through as a result of the actions the offender took against them.

But I also wonder, in contrast, if the victim has in turn considered what has led the one who injured them to do what they do and how they are now properly (or even in some cases, improperly) suffering the consequences of their actions as a result. And the question now begs itself from the distance--HAS JUSTICE TRULY BEEN SERVED FROM BOTH SIDES? Have BOTH sides truly comfortable now with the final results that they will now have to live with for the rest of their lives? AND--more importantly, is GOD satisfied with what has been decided? (Makes you think, doesn't it?)

Maybe at this middle point of this book, this would be the perfect time to say this: The time for games is over. The time for seeking vengeance and personal gain has now come to an end. Our God has now called us instead to start finding common ground with each other--to reconcile, to start (in essence) "walking a mile in someone else's moccasins". Instead of hostility and hatred towards each other, I honestly feel that God is now looking for us to love each other and start esteeming highly what God has decided to esteem highly--even if the other party in the natural doesn't seem to deserve it. Those of you on either side that think the other party is getting or has already got what deserve-let me ask you...did YOU deserve to be forgiven of your sins by our God? I'd dare say ABSOLUTELY NOT!! BUT He did so anyway for that exact reason--NOT for anything we might have done for Him, but ONLY because of His infinite grace and mercy. So why can we not think anything else even of the enemies and those who caused us so much grief and pain? Why must we be ashamed to love even those who do not feel loved or that did something so egregious to us that we should not ever forgive them, much less love them?

So I say let's spend this time together in this session focusing on a VERY necessary characteristic for both our recovery and personal growth. I think God wants to challenge us a little bit, stir up our nest a bit, and try to see things from the other side of the fence. I know this is a VERY hard thing to do--but until we get out of our self--centeredness and focus on the needs of someone else, the possibility that we may never truly heal from the trauma that surrounds us will still continue to be very real in our lives.

In one of my history classes I took when I was in college, the professor one time told us what seems to be a very relevant saying here: "Perception colors viewpoint." What he meant by this was that what you see, how you presume something to be, and how you perceive something will ultimately influence your overall viewpoint on any particular situation. I'd like to go into a little in-depth exploration of that saying by writing and comparing two different perspectives side-by-side--that of the offender and that of the victim. I'd like for all of us during this lesson to think as if you were NOT who you are now--BUT instead the OTHER person involved in the incident and how they see and view things. Maybe then in seeing how someone else walks in their moccasins will we get the fuller picture of why the other person is what he/she is.

First, let me talk to you victims on behalf of those who hurt you. Believe me, I DO NOT justify what they have done to you and that most might believe that they deserve what they have received from the justice system. But I would hope that you would balance your opinion with some very revealing information that might change the way you see that offender and cause you to think of them in a radically different light.

One of those victims might ask, "Well, why did they do what they did to me in the first place? Don't they know we have rules--and can't they obey them? WHY ME?? Why couldn't they have bothered someone else? Or better yet--why can't they just behave themselves (...or get a job like everyone else...or just act like everyone else in society...etc.)? One of the chapters of a training manual by Prison Fellowship might help shed a little light for the victim why that offender might be the way that he/she is right now. It cites some possible factors that might lead some to patterns of criminal behavior:

(1.) Abused as children
(2.) Dysfunctional families
(3.) Poor sense of self-worth
(4.) Racial minorities
(5.) Unrealistic outlooks

(6.)Suspicious nature
(7.) Alcohol and drug abuse
(8.) Poor readers
(9.) Unemployment
(10.) A bad rap

Victim, let me ask you this--has ANY one of these happened to you? If even ONE of them has, then you do have something in common with the one who hurt you after all. If not, then maybe this might force you to think twice before you start to hastily condemn them and refuse to forgive them for the action they took against you. NO-- this does NOT mean that you HAVE TO condone what they did--NOT IN THE LEAST!! Like it or not, that person who raped you, beat you, or did something terrible to you must still be forced to face the music for what they did to you--and you need to allow God to work his proper justice for them.

BUT you must temper those thoughts in a manner that shows mercy unto them--just as you have been shown mercy by others. YOU MUST NOT BE RULED BY ANGER, HURT, OR BITTERNESS in what you do--but instead you must be ruled SOLELY by what God and the Holy Spirit would have you to do and the attitude of love, mercy, and concern for the welfare of the other party involved. The reason you should testify in the courtroom against the person who hurt SHOULD NOT be for the sake of personal gain or vindication. To the contrary, you should do it as a way to confront the person who hurt you and force him/her to realize for the first time the pain that was brought to your doorstep as a result of their actions.

But if this does not hammer the point home to you victims about why prisoners are the way they are, maybe these statistics later on from that same training manual will help you walk in their moccasins a little bit and grasp for the first time why they might act in the way that they do:
***According to research, four out of five prisoners were abused as children either physically, sexually, and/or emotionally.
***Most of these prisoners come from families with serious shortcomings that have left deep wounds. Many had parents who abused themselves with drugs or alcohol. Many had parents who committed crimes. About 95% of all men in prison did not have a loving father figure in their home.
***Many prisoners have experienced failures in many areas: failure on a job, in relationships, in school, and even at crime. Failure--at least as we would define it-- has been a way of life. With no worthwhile successes, prisoners often boast of the only successes they have had--their crimes and their "tough skin".

***In the U.S., the lifetime chance of incarceration is six times higher for black males than for white males. In the 1980 U.S. census, blacks made up 12% of the average population. But, in 1984, 46% of the inmates in state prisons were black. In 1991 one of every four black men aged 20-29 was in prison or on probation or parole. The proportion of Hispanics in prisons and jails is also greater than in the total population. Many factors, including poverty, disadvantages, and discrimination, may contribute to this racial imbalance. Before arrest, the average inmate was living at the poverty level. Poverty compounds an accused person's problems if he or she cannot afford to hire a lawyer. And three-fourths of all defendants can't afford a private lawyer.

***Many prisoners are unrealistic about life and its many demands. Like children, they "want it NOW."...They may thrive on risk and adventure with little thought to the consequences of what they're doing. One study of habitual offenders reported that juveniles who went on to adult criminal careers gave these motives for crime: thrill-seeking, status, attention-getting, or peer influence. (As criminals aged, their reasons shifted to financial needs, especially for drugs or alcohol.)

***Chuck Colson, founder of Prison Fellowship, offers this comment about prisoners: "Most prisoners have been con-men on the outside. They live in an environment where conning is a way of life. Their lives are constantly manipulated by the prison staff, so they expect the same of you..."

***When he was U.S. attorney general, Edwin Meese said, "Overwhelming evidence now links drug use to criminal activity." He was commenting on a 1988 Department of Justice report: In 12 major cities, from 53 to 79% of the men arrested for serious offenses tested positive for illicit drugs.

***Several studies show that one out of five American adults cannot read well-enough to function in society; another shows
that one out of three is functionally illiterate. The Bureau of Justic estimates that almost 70% of all prisoners are functionally illiterate. Other studies put the figure at 80%. ***In 1989, 36% of all males in jail were unemployed at the time they entered jail. One researcher followed a group of ex-prisoners for 10 years after their release. The study found that 86% of the ex-prisoners who lasted less than one month on their first job after release were arrested again. The same study also showed that none of the former prisoners who stayed on that first job for a whole year were arrested in the next 10 years.

[Above information taken from "Behind The Wall: An Introduction To In-Prison Ministry"; Prison Fellowship Ministries; edited by Tammy Phillips, Dell Coats Erwin and Senior Editor Evelyn Bence; (C) 1990; p. 15-21.]

Victims, it's a harder row for a prisoner or offender to hoe than you think, eh? They aren't always in cushy country-club places like you think they might be. Instead, they are people that hurt just like you do, too. They have the same feelings, emotions, and heartaches you do. The only difference might be the types of barriers used to separate the two of you. Theirs just might happen to be razor wire and emotional pain; yours might be fear and a loss of a sense of trust and personal security. Otherwise, they hurt like you do: in different ways, yes--but nevertheless, they are in pain over you, too.

Now it's time to give equal time to the other side of the coin. Towards the end of Act II of Phantom of the Opera, as Raoul pleads for the Phantom to free Christine Dyae and let her return back to the Count, the Phantom roars back this response to him: "The world showed no compassion to me!" Maybe that statement serves as a lightning rod and a perfect transition point that might bring both the victim and the offender eventually to the point where the need for true and ultimate reconciliation becomes a deep-seated longing and desire for both parties AT THE RIGHT TIME AND ONLY IN GOD'S DIVINE SCHEME OF TIMING!!

Victims, what other thing could describe a possible rationale for why that criminal did what he/she did to you? COULD IT BE THAT NO COMPASSION OF ANY KIND HAS EVER BEEN SHOWN TO THEM AT ANY TIME DURING THE COURSE OF THEIR LIFE? Prisoners, why do you think the odds are stacked against you and why the system doesn't seem to show you any mercy and a desire to give you a second chance? Why won't people seem to believe you and think of you as being sincere when you say that you won't do what you did to the victim again? Why the vengeance against you? Why the hate and lack of compassion?

I know that so far I have rocked a few boats on one side of the ship--but that is probably because God might feel that it is DEFINITELY something that needs to be rocked. But now, I need to tilt the other side of the ship a little bit, too, in this process so that the whole premise of what I have to say will properly balance out.

Offender--why do you think that victim feels hurt, scared, and angry at the act that you had a part in doing? Why might society demand that you pay for your crimes and spend time in virtual slavery to pay restitution to the State for the problems you caused that other party? Why might people not have as much of a favorable opinion of you now because of what you did?

Let's first take a look at the classic parable of the Good Samaritan--BUT NOT in the way you would normally think. In three of the Gospels [Matt. 22:34-40; Mark 12:28-31; and Luke 10:25-37], this classic parable is usually regarded by most as the ultimate example of helping your fellow man in Christ's name--and rightfully so. But

I want to look at this from a totally different perspective.

Read these passages CLOSELY and tell me what you see here. WHY was the man described by our Savior in this parable stripped of his clothes, beaten, and left for dead? WHAT was so important about what the man had that these things could be so easily taken from him? And WHAT was the environment that all of this took place in?

Keener has something to tell about this in response in regards to Luke 10:30: "Like most parables, the story has one main point that answers the...question; the details are part of the story and are not meant to be allegorized. Jericho was lower in elevation than Jerusalem; hence one would "go down" there. Robbers were common along the road and would especially attack a person traveling alone. Many people did not have extra clothes, which were thus a valuable item to steal."

DID YOU READ THAT? The man ended up in this terrible situation BECAUSE HE WAS ROBBED--i.e., HE WAS VICTIMIZED!! Now let me ask you BOTH--WHY does a robber steal? WHY are the things that someone else has that we covet more valuable than what we already carry on our person? WHY is a victim so helpless and dependent on others to do what he/she cannot do for himself/herself? WHY is a victim usually reluctant to get himself/herself out of an abusive situation? WHY do BOTH the victim and the offender seem so hopeless, despondent, depressed, unable to cope with life, and trapped by circumstances that seem to be out of their control? I can tell you this much--it certainly AIN'T because they don't have the motivation to do so! One can wish and desire and dream to do something all day, night, and even all of the rest of their life--but if one does not take those steps to put those things into action, that something will only remain at best an unreachable dream that will never come true.

Now prisoners--pay special attention to the remainder of the passage. Did you notice that BECAUSE the robbery took place the man needed help from someone else to do what he couldn't do for himself? Now, let me ask you another question--if the man HAD NOT been robbed, would he have needed that help from someone else? OF COURSE NOT!! Now let's take this thing even further and see for ourselves what might have happened IF this crime HAD NOT taken place:

(1.) The injured WOULD NOT have been beaten, WOULD NOT have been stripped of his clothes, and certainly WOULD NOT have been left for dead. He would probably be walking, talking, and doing those things that he was originally intending to do in the first place.

103

(2.) TWO religious officials WOULD NOT have been in danger of becoming ritually unclean and therefore automatically considered being fit to serve in the services of the Temple.

(3.) No Samaritan would have had to take care of the injured man. He would have NOT had to take time from his busy schedule or spend money out of his own pocket to take care of a man that was harmed by someone else who wanted to take advantage of him and had to fix what someone else had screwed up.

(4.) (This one I found REAL funny.) The innkeeper wouldn't have had to be responsible for one more guest at his business AND CERTAINLY would have NOT had one more opportunity to make money off of someone else's misery.

(5.) Our Savior couldn't have been able to describe what true mercy to others really is otherwise and there would have NOT been an interesting story to tell us that is in the pages of the Bible that we read. And worse than that, there would be less of the Word that we would be able to read and less of an opportunity to know the true character and nature of what our Savior truly is.

And you say, "And you got all of this from a simple account about highway robbery?" Yes, I did. But that's nothing compared to some other stuff that I am about to tell you about from TWO different perspectives: that of a victim of a crime myself AND also that of a member of a Grand Jury.

First, let me share with you (ESPECIALLY those of you who are prisoners) a FIRSTHAND experience of what it's like to be a victim of a "misdeameanor" crime. One night about 4 or 5 AM, I was awakened by a knock on the door of my apartment. When I opened the door, there on my front steps stood two Black ladies, one of them who I had seen on two previous occasions and that had asked me for various
things, and the other who was pretty overweight. When I opened the door, one of them asked me if I could give them money for a bus ticket to a nearby town. When I told them I didn't have it, then the lady asked if I could fix them a glass of water. After I let them in, I fixed the glasses of water and them gave them to the ladies--in which they left pretty quickly afterwards and I turned off the light and went back to sleep.

The next morning, I tried to find my cell phone and tore the house up and down looking for it--but couldn't find it. Then I had the idea that I might have left it at a church I had went to the previous night for a singles group. So I took some time to go to that church to find the phone that I thought I might have misplaced there-- and came up with zero. After going down the exact trail I had walked the night before, only then did I realize that those same ladies that I had let in during the night may have also stolen my phone. All of which caused me to go to the agent for the cell phone company I was using at the time to get a replacement phone...which then required me to file a police report...which then afterwards required me to go back to the cell phone company to pick up the replacement phone. A whole day wasted on my part due to the actions of someone else...

But what really got my goat was this: I was virtually dependent on that phone in order to keep my job and maintain all appropriate contact with the outside world. But what was that phone worth to those ladies? I soon found out after one of the city police officers told me what eventually happened to that phone. The police had found that phone just blocks away from my apartment in an nearby park. What did the ladies get for the trouble of stealing my phone? To them, it was a quick high of an illegal drug and quick cash to do something stupid. To me, it cost a whole lot more in terms of time spent trying to rectify this situation and inconvienence and hassle in having to replace a phone and then having to return the replacement phone and get the original phone that I had back in operation again.

Through this little episode, though, God also showed me a deeper lesson. At most, I only lost out through crime in terms of time and inconvienence. BUT PRISONERS--HAVE YOU EVER EVEN IMAGINED the harm you may have caused someone when you commit a crime? Look back at some of the chapters in Unit II and think about how your crimes (ESPECIALLY those involving in some form domestic violence and/or sexual assault) affect the victim.

BUT ALSO REMEMBER THAT A CRIME DOES NOT JUST AFFECT ONE PERSON!! Keep in mind that your crimes cost us more to keep you housed, fed, and incarcerated now. It costs YOU the ability for you to even find a job once you are released (if you ever are, that is) because it will be VERY hard for us on the outside to trust you and give you the second chance that you might want to start out new and get back on your own two feet. It costs your FAMILIES in terms of financial problems and additional stress and strain on their relationships with you and makes it harder for them to keep in touch with you now. And it costs the TAXPAYERS of the place where you live more in money that they have to pay for the government to pay for YOUR attorney, YOUR right to a fair trial, YOUR stay as a ward of the State. AND it costs our GOD the ability to use His power and strength in your life to create an opportunity for a blessing and a miracle in your life. (Man, that little thing you did--sure costs you and everyone else a lot more than you think...)

But who is forced to pay an even higher price for what you did to that victim? GUESS WHAT--it IS the victim himself/herself! If you look back on the Good

Samaritan parable, the obvious becomes a whole lot easier to see. It COSTS the one you harmed valuable time from work because of the injuries you caused. IT COSTS THEM extra expense that they had to incur because you were not willing to restrain yourself from doing what you did. IT COSTS THEM the peace of mind that these folks used to have about their surroundings. IT COSTS THEM in terms of their personal sense of security and sense of well-being. IT COSTS THEM in terms of their ability to put their trust in others and to have confidence in ANYTHING a particular person says or does to them. IT COSTS THEM in terms of problems that they now face in being able to have meaningful relationships with others. IN SHORT--your crime has cost them A WHOLE LOT more to them than it should. And they usually did NOT have ANYTHING to do with it and DID NOT do anything to deserve that fate.

I saw this a lot in my experiences as a Grand Juror. The victim pays a lot because of additional and unexpected medical expenses that they cannot pay for and in the loss of things that they once held dear due to things that they absolutely had no control over. You, the offender, in contrast, pay by losing the respect of those who once respected you and the trust of all of society that once trusted you. SO let's ask if crime truly does pay. Based on experience, I would safely venture to say that it does not.

But for those of you who are offenders who still are not convinced of the deep and lasting impact that a crime can have on a victim, then I would ask that you read closely the words of Darrell Scott, the father of Columbine High School shooting victim Rachel Scott, and see for yourself if and how the actions of a person can deeply affect in some way the lives of someone else:

"...We continue our special report this week from the Worldview Weekend Conference with what probably was its biggest capstone highlight--the time when Darrell Scott, the father of Rachel Scott, one of the fatalities of the tragedy that occurred...at Columbine High School in Littleton, CO, shared his heart with conference participants about the experiences he and his family have went through. It is amazing to note that the anniversary of the shooting will occur in just a little more than two weeks from now--and one would naturally think that a father like Mr. Scott would have just reasons to be bitter and resentful about what happened. But apparently Mr. Scott feels otherwise and prefers to express what might be to some very totally different and radical statements about the reasons for his daughter's death...

"...To illustrate how people these days might recall the Columbine tragedy, Scott asked for the number of participants who remembered what they were doing when the assasination of President John F. Kennedy occurred. "...If you asked them what they were doing on November 22, 1963, they can tell you because something happened that caused the clock to stop and for time to stand still...This [the Columbine tragedy] was the equivalent to this generation...to the John F. Kennedy and Martin Luther King assasinations of my generation." He also emphasized his view that the Columbine tragedy was a spiritual event--one that he was forced to live through personally.

"...Scott also related the memory he had of when he was caught in the massive traffic jam towards an elementary school in which was packed full of parents and families waiting to see if their children had survived the shooting. As their loved ones waited, the children were marched across the stage as their name was called--in which were greeted with screams of joy and were then able to leave the building with their families. "And to watch that crowd begin to dwindle slowly after bus after bus after bus had come and then to be told there was one bus left--and I don't think I'll ever again in my life have that kind of experience to hear the announcement, "There's only one bus left."--to me, that was the epitome of the horror that I personally felt...and feeling a mixture of anticipation, of hope, and yet of deep, deep dread that I may never see my daughter alive again," Scott related to the attendees.

"...Scott also publicly thanked those present for their prayers and support during the crisis and its aftermath on behalf of all of the families affected by Columbine. He also remarked that the shooting didn't start on April 20th--but instead long before that in the worldviews and hearts of Eric Harris and Dylan Klebold. He cited the example of when he saw the videotapes that Eric and Dylan had made two months before when they talked about "...starting a chain reaction"--a statement chillingly and hauntingly similar to one Rachel had made in challenging her classmates in an assignment to "...start a chain reaction with acts of kindness"--that the elder Scott feels that it has made this generation more clearly see "...how we galvanize in this generation the evil and good. It's time for us to make a decision; it's time for us to come out of the closet." Scott also noted in the tapes that Eric and Dylan had made that the two boys blasted Christianity and had even mentioned Rachel by name as a specific target of their future attack.

"...Scott also noted an instance of a lady who drove by the school thousands of times on here way to work had, on the morning of the shooting, felt impressed for unknown reasons to pray for the school for about one hour that morning and came to work late as a result. As well, he mentioned that a prayer group at Columbine (which was the largest one in the whole state) had actually prayed that God would use their school mightily to reach people in their country and that three months prior to the incident Bruce Porter (a part-time firefighter and pastor) had a very vivid disturbing dream that would foreshadow what might come at the school (in which he would later preside over the funeral of the victims in a live television broadcast that garnered the highest audience that CNN ever had in his history at that time).

"Later in the presentation, Scott, in the midst of reading one of the entries of Rachel's diary, posed a question in the minds of conference participants by saying, "...Rachel prayed a prayer--she said, "God, I want you to use me to reach the unreached." How many of you ever prayed prayers and God answered those prayers--but he didn't answer them the way you thought He should answer them?" Scott illustrated the point by noting what he felt the ways that God provides patience and then told participants something that a good friend who had an impact on his life had told him, "Darrell, learn how to be a see-througher and not a look-ater...If you don't become a see-througher, if you are a look-ater, you are going to live in defeat and frustration in your Christian walk. But if you will learn to see through things to the reality that's behind this world, you will live in fruitfulness and you will never, ever see anything except what's behind the visage."--something that would prove to be helpful in dealing with the aftermath of the Columbine tragedy.".........

"Last week, we discussed some of the highlights of a speech given by Darrell Scott, father of Columbine H.S. shooting victim Rachel Scott and founder of the Columbine Redemption, at the American Family Policy Institute's recent Worldview Weekend conference here. We managed to ask Mr. Scott a few quick questions after his presentation. Here's what he had to say:

Suite 101: Mr. Scott, a question that's probably on our reader's minds a lot--what, more than anything else, could have caused Columbine? And how can we prevent it from happening again?

Scott: I think that's a very complex answer--and I think that there's a number of things that we do need to look at. One of them is easy accessibility of guns, obviously. Another is the fact that there was parental neglect, it appears--I don't want t o be pointing any fingers, but we don't spend as much time with our kids as we did back in the '50s and '60s with two parents working most of the time.

But I think one of the big areas is that our teachers, our principals, and even parents have not been allowed the freedom to bring discipline to our children like they used to--so they're afraid to bring any discipline. And on the other hand, we've removed all spiritual input and all spiritual influence to our children from our schools. And ultimately, we can't have all of these things happening without some negative results. I see it as a compilation of a number of things--but two of the big areas is the fact that we've had our hands tied in discipline; and on the other hand, we've had no spiritual input to our kids.

101: Also, I'm wondering what, more than anything else, would be the legacy of this event? What do you feel will be the legacy will be for years to come?

Scott: I believe that Columbine was a wake-up call spiritually to this generation. Other people won't agree with that--but that's my very strong belief because of the things that happened--and I'm one of the closest people to the tragedy. And I've se en the results already--and many of the results have been positive...And I think that it will go down in history as a turning point for our country and our conscience.

"...We thought that as the upcoming anniversary of the Littleton tragedy approaches that you might wish to see the transcript of the last part of Mr. Scott's speech as a way to wrap this conference up in a nutshell.

Sometimes in journalism, reporters tend to spend so much time asking questions that the very words that a person says to an assembly are sometimes lost in the shuffle. Due to space restraints and time limitations, it is obviously very hard to print it all. But we thought it best to let you read for yourself for a while something directly from the horse's mouth--and let the words of someone who went through it do the talking for a while. We pick up the speech from the point after Mr. Scott has finished briefly memorializing all of the victims who died in the shooting:

"Now I want to end with this--I want you to see in her [Rachel's] handwriting the last poem that my daughter wrote. It has a prophetic tone concerning the Columbine tragedy. She wrote it about her relationship with God and about her school. She says,

'Am I the only one who sees?
Am I the only one who craves Your glory?
Am I the only one who longs to be forever
in Your loving arms?
All I want is for someone to walk with me
through these halls of a tragedy.
Please give me a loving friend who will carry Your Name until the end,
Someone who longs to be with you,

someone who will stay forever true.'

"I got such comfort in finding Cassie's [Bernall] name in Rachel's room because I believe God answered that prayer, too. You know that she named 13 people in her diaries that she was praying for--and all 13 of those people have come to know Jesus since her death? She prayed, 'God, use me to reach the unreached.'--and God has answered that prayer over and over again and will continue to answer that prayer over and over again. She prayed, 'Give me someone to walk with me through these halls of a tragedy.'--and she met Cassie a few nights before she died. And she parked her car about three or four car lengths away from John Tomlins--and we'd like to think that maybe that morning on the way into the school, their paths crossed and they greeted one another. But God did answer every prayer that Rachel prayed.

"...I want to end with this--and this is the most remarkable story of the Columbine tragedy that I know personally; it's the one that changed my life so radically. It caused me to believe that God has an anointing on this next generation that's coming up . And I said before Congress, 'My daughter's death will not be in vain--the young people of this nation will not allow that to happen.' And I said it on the conviction of something that I'm about to share with you.

"...A month after Rachel's death, I was settling into my bed and I said, 'God, I'll do what you want me to do. Two requests--You have to open the doors and I want to wear blue jeans.' And I meant what I prayed. As soon as I prayed that prayer, a minute or so later, my phone rang and I picked it up--and it was a gentleman by the name of Frank Omenia--a man I'd never met before, never heard of. He's very wealthy, he owns businesses across America--if I named his company, some of you would recognize the name.

"He said, 'Mr. Scott, you don't know who I am. I have watched your daughter's funeral. I am a Christian--and I was so moved.' And he said, 'God put a burden on my heart for you and let me know to pray for you because I believe that he's going to raise you up to speak to young people and leaders across this nation.' That was what he said to me. It was such a confirmation in my heart of what God was already speaking to me.

"...And so he said, 'But that's not the reason I'm calling. The reason I'm calling you is, first of all, I want to let you know that I am going to help financially support what you do because I believe that God's going to put His hand on you to make a difference.' But he said, 'The reason I'm calling you is because three times in my life I have had dreams that I knew were from God.' He said, 'I'm not a mystical person--

and I don't put a lot of stock in dreams and visions.' But he said, "Three times I've had dreams I knew without a shadow of a doubt were from God. The first two had to do with my company, my business--and in both cases, what I dreamed came to pass after a period of time. God blessed my businesses; they prospered; I've been able to give liberally to different ministry works.'

"...And he said, 'The third dream is the most powerful that I have ever had--and I know it's from the Lord and I want you to help me understand what it means.' He said, 'I've dreamed about your daughter's eyes; and there's tears flowing out of her eyes and they're watering something--but I can't see what it is.' He said, 'Do you know what that means?' I said, 'Frank, I don't have any idea what.' He said, 'Well, I used to play in a band with Alice Cooper before I became a Christian, played keyboards. I'm writing a song called 'Rachel's Tears'"...Michael W. Smith will be with us on April 20th; and that song may be sung at that memorial service that Frank has written--it's a beautiful song...But he said, "I've written a song called 'Rachel's Tears ' and I want to give it to young people around the country that I have influence with. If that ever means anything to you, please let me know because I see her eyes and I see a stream of tears and I see them watering something--but I don't know what it is.' I said, "If it ever means anything, Frank, I'll be glad to call you.'

"...I wrote his number down, kind of forgot about it about two or three days later. And seven days later, I got a phone call from the sheriff's department. They said, "It's time to come pick up the things that were in your daughter's backpack." We knew they were holding some items because there was a bullet hole in the backpack that went through this diary--and she had her last diary as well in that backpack. I rushed over, got the things that were wrapped up in white plastic, took them out to my truck, sat down...And I just can't describe what it's like to read something knowing that it's the last thing that she wrote. I took her final diary, opened it up to the last page--and what I saw was absolutely the most startling thing that's ever happened to me in my life. I sat there stunned for 35 to 40 minutes--I could not even move. And I began to weep and I prayed, "God, you've got to help me understand what I'm looking at."-- and what you're about to see in the last picture is what I saw."

(Refers to video screen) "...When I saw this picture in Rachel's diary on the last page, I found out later that she drew this 30 minutes before she died. [Editor's Note: Scott is referring to an image on the screen described as mentioned below.] Her friend Sarah Arizzola saw her drawing this and she said that she was drawing as though her life depended on it. Someone pointed out to me later that there's 13 clear tears falling from her eyes before they touched the rose that turned dark. There were 13 victims 30 minutes after she drew these pictures that died from the guns of Eric and Dylan.

And as I sat there looking at that picture, I was absolutely stunned. I'm thinking, "God, there's a stranger that's calling me up that's had a vision or a dream about what I'm looking at--and I'm praying tonight--I want you to help me understand what this means if this means something.'

"...The Lord spoke to my heart as clearly as I've ever heard him speak. He said, 'That rose represents the young people of this generation.' And I remembered that that same rose was the one connected to a picture she had drawn months before. It was growing up out of a columbine plant and it was connected to a verse of Scripture that said, "Greater love hath no man than this: that a man lay down his life for his friends." And as I sat in my truck and wept, the Lord gently spoke to my heart and said, "Rachel's death is not in vain. Those are not just her tears--those are My tears. I am raising this generation up--and out of this tragedy, I have touched their hearts. I'm anointing them with My own tears to do a work that I have called them to do that your generation and the generations before you haven't done.'

"...That was so clear to me. I shared that about a month later when I spoke in Jackson, TN to 5,000 people at an open field. And a young girl came up to me with her Bible and she was crying and she said, "Mr. Scott, I didn't know what you were going to t alk about today. But three nights ago, I was reading in my Bible--and God spoke to me about some verses in Jeremiah. I want you to read this.' She handed me her Bible. And it was turned to Jeremiah 31:15-17...and this is what it says:

"...This is what the Lord says: A voice is heard in Ramah, mourning and great weeping, Rachel weeping for her children and refusing to be comforted because her children are no more...This is what the Lord says:' Restrain your voice from weeping and your eyes for tears--for your work will be rewarded,' declares the Lord. They, the children, will return from the land of the enemy. So there is hope for your future," declares the Lord. Your children will return to their own land." Some translations say "...their own inheritance."

"...When I read those words, it was like a door slammed shut in my heart of closure. And from that moment on, I would not ask for my daughter to be brought back. If that sounds cruel or heartless or unfatherly, I ask your forgiveness. But I wouldn't because I knew from that moment on, I've never doubted that Rachel was born for a purpose. And God prepared her heart and her life for that moment on April 20th when she would be killed and that from her diaries young people's lives would be touched. And Rachel would be angry with me if I brought her back because she could live to be 500 years old and never have had the impact that she's had. Her prayers have been answered--God has reached the unreached through my daughter's death.

"...I want to end by saying this--it cost me everything. The most pain that I could ever possibly have in my life has already happened. There's nothing you can do to me that could be worse than what has already been done. It cost me a lot to be where I'm at. And I'm here on a mission--and that mission is: Let's don't go about our Christian life and put business as usual. I'm here to challenge you tonight--let some of the words from beyond the grave, from some of these young people who were fervent in their zeal and love for God and laid their lives down because they believed what they believe. And I do believe that Columbine was a spiritual event..."

There's probably one final question that we got to ask Mr. Scott that might say it all:

101: And what might probably be a more apt question than anything else--what now from here? Where does it all go--where does it all lead?

Scott: Well, I think different people are going to go different directions. I can only answer that for myself personally--and that is, it has changed my life and I'm dedicated to the memory of my daughter to making a difference in our high schools in our nation by speaking to young people, getting involved with legislation--which I'm doing, and just by doing everything within my power to make a difference. That's all any one person can do--to the degree that God opens the doors and you step through them.
[The previous sections taken from previous articles by the author at Suite 101.com (now defunct), (C) 2000. All rights reserved. Used by permission.]

Our Savior says from the mountain. "Why do you look at the speck of sawdust in your brother's eye and pay no attention to the plank in your own eye? How can you say to your brother, 'Let me take the speck out of your eye,' when all the time there is a plank in your own eye? You hypocrite, first take the plank out of your own eye, and then you will see clearly to remove the speck from your brother's eye." (Matt. 7:3-5)

I can only add this to Mr. Scott's most eloquent words--don't just take the plank out of your own eye, but then walk a mile in someone else's moccasins, too, while you're at it. Get a true feeling for what it's like for the other party to go through what they go through. Victims--understand what led that offender to do what they did to you. Offenders--face up to the consequences of your actions and see for once the harm and devastation you might have caused someone else. Don't just take the plank out of the eye, but walk at least TWO miles in the other's shoes as well. Then maybe the view from the other side of the fence will seem a whole lot clearer to you and you will realize how much more common ground you might actually have. And that's probably a whole lot more than you think.

[DISCUSSION QUESTIONS:]

(1.) Discuss IN DETAIL what it would be like to be a victim if you are an offender (and if, in contrast, you are a victim--then what it's like to be a prisoner/offender). Then role-play in some way a day in the life of that person.
(2.) Go through a quick character study of the Parable of the Good Samaritan in Luke 10. Who are the major figures that you see in it and what does each of them act like? WHY would you imagine that they would act like they do?
(3.) About the earlier list of common reasons why criminals commit crimes, discuss what things that victims and criminals might have in common about that list. In what ways might each be the same? In what ways would you imagine they are different?
(4.) Go back and look at the Darrell Scott articles that are a part of this lesson and what happened at Columbine. What would you imagine ran through the minds of some of the victims such as Rachel Scott and Cassie Bernall at the time of the shooting? What about the killers, Eric Harris and Dylan Klebold? What about ALL of the parents of those in the high school and the community of Littleton, CO before, during, and after the infamous shooting? How could it relate to what we might be discussing here in regards to the relationship between victims and offenders?

[PRAYER:] Creator Father, Lord God Almighty, and Lord Jesus/Y'shua: This was a painful lesson for me to learn, but nevertheless thank you for teaching it to me. Thank you for forcing me to see my need to look beyond myself and see how it is truly like from the other side of the fence. Thank you for impressing upon me the importance of trying to understand and grasp what it is like to "walk a mile in someone else's shoes". Lord, help me NEVER to forget this lesson and to make sure that BEFORE I do something that is inappropriate to others and that is not pleasing and glorifying to You that I would first take the time necessary to consider how the decision that I might make would affect others. Then help me to make RIGHT decisions and take RIGHT actions that would BLESS others and not harm or hurt them in any way. Lord, I want to be a blessing to others and not a pain or a curse to them. Help me to use this lesson as a tool that would make it easier for me to do so. I ask this in Your Son's Name--AMEN!!

UNIT III, LESSON 3--The Berlin Wall of Hostility and Separation

Do you recall or remember when the Berlin Wall fell in Germany? I do VERY well--for I got to sit and watch it fall right in front of my eyes right in the TV lounge of my dorm when I went to Eastern New Mexico University. I was distressed over this event, but mainly for different reasons than you think (none of which are relevant to talk about in this particular lesson). But I recall the men who took sledgehammers to the Wall and broke up the concrete that stood at one time between one part of Germany and the other and the people who drank champagne and partied for what seemed like forever and celebrating the fact that after many years of repression, poverty, senseless losses of life, and brutal dictatorship--they were finally free for what was for some the VERY first time in their lives. ("...Kingdoms may rise and kingdoms may fall, but the word of the LORD will stand forever...")

But one might imagine what those folks had to go through in the years before the Wall finally fell. How did they even manage to eek out a bare living? How did they manage to survive without freedom of speech and other things that Americans like myself might tend to take for granted? What about the painful scars and memories that they now carry from their past experiences? And how now do they live in what might soon be for them extremely turbulent times that will be even more uncertain than before? And how can these folks forgive those that tormented them for so many years and avoid the urge to retaliate against their former tormentors in inappropriate and excessive ways?

I don't know about what the future about the nation of Germany here--and besides, that is NOT the purpose of this lesson anyway. Instead, I just might wish to use these questions as foundational stepping stones to deal with the Berlin Walls of hostility and separation that we build in our relationships with others--ESPECIALLY as a result of lives damaged and scarred by physical, emotional, mental, and sexual abuse of any kind. Let's use this lesson to evaluate ourselves and see if there be any fault or anything that we might still have lurking deep inside us.

Now to start this, let me make myself clear on a thing or two BEFORE we get into this subject of hostility and separation. FIRST--if YOU personally are in a situation of ANY kind in which you might face imminent danger or that might otherwise cause you to compromise your faith in God in order to reconcile yourself to someone else or that will only put you back in a situation of never-ending misery, THIS DOES NOT MEAN that you must be a doormat to everyone else's whims in order for your problems to be totally resolved. HEAVEN FORBID THAT IT WOULD BE SO!

Prudent caution, wisdom, and guidance are things I HIGHLY advise that you use to also take care of yourself in these situations. ALSO--don't expect that what follows is the ONLY cause for the problems you face. What I offer here is only at best one mere additional step that you might wish to take within your recovery process and that ONLY you and God can ultimately decide what is in your best interests. But maybe if we take a little time to explore these issues here at this point in our studies, it might to prove to be a blessing and benefit to us.

Let's start by considering what might be some common reasons why these Berlin Walls of hostility and separation might get built in the first place. What might you possibly imagine they might be?

POSSIBLE REASONS FOR BUILDING THE BERLIN WALLS THAT SEPARATE US:

(1.) MISCOMMUNICATION AND MISUNDERSTANDINGS--This is probably one of the biggies right here. We all have different ways of relating to each other, different personality traits, and different stations of life that we each live in. We might not have heard something that another person said (remember the Bradley model of communication in Unit II, Lesson I?) or find ourselves in situations in which we haven't fully concentrated on what that other person REALLY meant and said.

(2.) DIFFERENT MANNERS OF UPBRINGING AND ENVIRONMENT--Look for instance at how even women cook differently from each other. Some don't cook at all; others only just a little bit as they need to; and still more do this all the time. They also have different methods of cooking. THE EXACT recipe that one mom taught to her daughter WILL NOT be the same that some other mom taught to her child. It sometimes is simply a matter of the differences and learned prejudices of other people.

(3.) UNRESPONSIVENESS OF THE OTHER PARTY--Sometimes silence can be interpreted by someone as indirectly expressed anger or hostility. To some, silence might be golden--but to others, it might as well mean the start of a cold war between two individuals that might escalate even further should any cross remarks cross the lips of one of the affected parties.

(4.) PERCEIVED MISTREATMENT OF ONE PARTY BY THE OTHER--One party can feel that they have been mistreated by another and decide to retaliate by withholding love, affection, or something else from the other party in order to "get back at them".

(5.) INAPPROPRIATE ACTING OUT OF OFFENSIVE BEHAVIORS--When someone acts in a manner that is not pleasing to others or that may cause anger, hostility, or bitterness to take root in a person's life, the separation and hatred grows thicker and thicker with time.

The relation of these Berlin Walls to the problems of domestic violence and sexual abuse, you ask? I'm not exactly sure about this--but I wonder if my God is trying to show me and you that the process of your eventual recovery from these situations will NOT be complete in His eyes and cannot come to a full resolution UNLESS and UNTIL these Berlin Wall obstacles of hostility and separation are torn down and UNLESS and UNTIL we allow God to start HIS divinely-ordained process of forgiveness, restitution, and reconciliation to begin.

Maybe an illustration or two might further prove my point. Earlier in the day before writing this lesson, I faced a situation in which I received an e-mail from one of my co-pastors regarding my behavior after church services on a certain situation. He told me in no uncertain terms that I had acted rudely and inappropriately within that situation. It is in those type of situations where it seems a thousand various thoughts (good and bad) can come into your mind. The major challenge in this for me is answering this question: How do I properly process those thoughts in a manner that is pleasing to God?

I could theorectically do this in different ways. I could take offense at this remark by my co-pastor and say something rash back to him in response. Or I could, if I wanted to, let his statement go, BUT start inwardly resenting him in my heart and disrespect his position and place of leadership that God has ordained him into (and therefore turning inwardly bitter). I could cry and manipulate and beg and plead and try to get my way and force my agenda on him. OR I could try to shift the blame and attempt to justify my actions. I could think of a NUMBER of ways that I could respond to a remark like that in a negative manner.

OR I COULD CHOOSE TO think of him in a more positive light. I might decide to respectfully disagree with him, but be willing to tolerate his views and/or respect his high place and position regardless of what he wishes to say. (But then it would only be simply politeness--NOT love!) I could instead begin to question myself (NOT, of course, in a way that causes me to go through unnecessary self-doubt) and ask, "Am I truly doing something wrong? Is there something inside myself that I need to change? Does he seem to have a valid point and is this a thing that I need to hear and respond to?" I could also entertain the thought that my co-pastor made the remark primarily out of concern for my well-being and welfare as well as that of the rest of the congregation.

Whatever or however these Berlin Walls are built, the God that I serve DOES NOT intend for them to remain up forever. Sooner or later, they will also have to come crashing down on your head, too. God's ultimate purpose and desire is that "...so from now on we regard no one from a worldly point of view. Though we once regarded Christ in this way, we do so no longer. Therefore, if anyone is in Christ, he is a new creation; the old has gone, the new has come! All this is from God, who reconciled us to himself through Christ and gave us the ministry of reconciliation.: that God was reconciling the world to himself in Christ, not counting men's sins against them. And he has committed to us the message of reconciliation. We are therefore Christ's ambassadors, as though God were making his appeal through us. We implore you on Christ's behalf: Be reconciled to God. God made him who had no sin to be sin for us, so that in him we might become the righteousness of God..." (2 Corinthians 5:16-21)

Keener has something interesting to say here in dealing with the last part of the above passage and how he equates the treatment of an ambassador or messenger who is sent by some prominent official to represent the official's interests:

> "Having established that he and his colleagues are Christ's representatives, Paul entreats the Corinthian Christians to be reconciled to God again by being reconciled again to himself...treatment of a herald reflected one's attitude toward the sender...

> "An 'ambassador' was a representative of one state to another, usually applied in this period to the emperor's legates in the East. This image fits 'apostles' as appointed messengers...just as the Old Testament prophets has been (Exodus 7:1)...In the context of a plea for reconciliation, Paul as an ambassador urges the Corinthians to make peace with God the King; emperors normally took action against unrepentant client states that had offended them, and no one took such warnings lightly...Here Paul means that Christ became sin's representative when he bore its judgment on the cross, and Paul and his associates become righteousness's representatives when they proclaim his message..."

If the Lord of the Universe has literally laid prostrate on the ground before us begging us to come back to him and showing his willingness to do what he felt it would take just so that we could be convinced of doing so--then how much more should we be willing to break down those Berlin Walls of hostility and separation that obscure our view of the rest of the world and prevent us from truly being what we should be from Him!!

As I said earlier, I DON'T claim to know exactly what you have personally walked through. But I am here to tell you now that it WILL NOT matter what you have walked through--UNLESS AND UNTIL you do your part to tear down these walls...YOU WILL NEVER TRULY HEAL COMPLETELY!! I DON'T PARTICULARLY CARE what has been done to you--you WILL NOT recover for sure until this cancer of hostility is COMPLETELY removed from your being, until all bitterness has entirely evaporated, AND until your walls of separation and loneliness are replaced with the fresh air and open fields of closeness, intimacy, and true fellowship with both your Creator and with others around you.

Something in my spirit right now senses that there is some form of hostility, bitterness, and separation of some kind that you're possibly holding on to...some form of bitterness or painful memories that you just can't quite let go of. The God that I serve is telling you RIGHT NOW that for His name's sake--LET IT GO....LET IT ALL GO!! Don't let these chains called resentment, strife, bitterness, and sorrow hold you down ANY LONGER!! LET IT GO, I SAY!! LET IT GO!! WHAT??? YOU SAY THAT YOU CAN'T OR DON'T KNOW HOW TO???

Maybe part of the reason might be that you haven't fully experienced God's goodness, mercy, and grace for yourself. If the REAL problem is the fact that you DO NOT yet have a CLOSE, INTIMATE, AND SATISFYING relationship with your Creator Father, then I would urge you to turn back to the section on salvation earlier in this book BEFORE moving on with this lesson. Until you take that first step, it will be MUCH harder to take the steps that follow. I WILL NOT guarantee by any means that this will be a magic cure for anything--but I DO BELIEVE that God CAN AND WILL use what is our PRAYER for today to bring about some MAJOR changes in your life that will bless you and restore you.

One time, I was in a situation that involved these very issues when I saw the "Hour of Healing" on TV featuring Richard and Lindsey Roberts. On this one particular night, I watched what has proved to me to be a very interesting revelation on what God truly thinks the term 'forgiveness' is. I like to call it the "Lindsay Roberts 2-Step

Forgiveness Formula". Read the following CLOSELY--for I feel it will truly change your life.

She basically said that forgiveness is NOT a matter of saying "I forgive you" and that's that. NO--forgiveness involves MUCH MORE than that. She suggests this:

"When you pray to Father God, you say: 'Father God, in the name of Jesus--I acknowledge that this person has done something that is terribly wrong to me and the harm that has been done in my life. Now, Father God, I now want to let you know that I forgive this person for what has been done to me and release them unto You as you would do with them.'

Now most people only end and stop there. When you forgive that other person and release them to God, God is then obligated to deal with them in judgment. But then there is a problem...the Word of God also says that "...if you will not forgive others, how can you expect the Father in Heaven to forgive you?'" When Christ died on the cross, he was not only your sacrifice for sin--but He also served as your Advocate before the Father in Heaven asking Him not to deal with them in judgment, but instead to deal with you in His mercy.

"God wants you to also stand in the gap for the person who wronged you--to be their attorney before Him in the manner of Christ. Then when you intercede and stand in the gap for that other person, you actually now allow God to deal with them in His mercy and love and you can actually be free of the chains that have bound you."

I personally couldn't have thought of a better way to talk about the BIBLICAL model of forgiveness myself. Why don't YOU pray this prayer to God and BE FREE OF THESE CHAINS INDEED? FREE FROM THE PAST THAT HAS BOUND YOU--FREE FROM THE SHACKLES AND CHAINS OF PAST EMOTIONAL WOUNDS AND HURTS THAT HAVE TIED YOU DOWN!!! DOESN'T THAT SOUND GREAT TO YOU??? Now it doesn't matter whether or not the person that has wronged in ANY matter (whether it might be incest or physical abuse or whatever it is)--you can STILL forgive in absentia and not be bound by the past that has haunted you. Pray this prayer RIGHT NOW:

PRAYER: Creator Father, God Almighty, and Lord Jesus/Y'shua: I come to You now about someone who has hurt me deeply and has done something terrible to me. (Name that person!) has done something that has scarred me forever. But in spite of the pain, I want to come before You now to ask the following:

First, I know that (name of person) has hurt me and has caused me much grief, pain, and sorrow. But I want you to know right now that just as you have forgiven me, I also now forgive _____ for what has been done to me and now release them to you to do as you desire--but NOT in my will, but Yours.

BUT NOT ONLY THAT, LORD---but I also now come before you interceding and pleading on behalf of _____ as their advocate before you to ask that you would not hold what they have done against me to their account and that you would also forgive them as well for what they have done to me and that you would be merciful to them, a fellow sinner just like me, so that you can deal with them in your great mercy and love. I also repent of any bitterness, ill feelings, and other things that are not of You and ask that you would take them out of my life RIGHT NOW!! And also, release me from these chains that have bound me for so long so that I can now more fully serve you with my whole heart--even more than I ever have before. In your Son's name I pray--AMEN!

DISCUSSION QUESTIONS:
(1.) Did you pray the prayer that is listed above? How did you feel after you prayed that prayer to the Lord? What do you feel about the person who wronged you now?

(2.) What does the Apostle Paul possibly have to say about the subject of hostility and division and separation? Read Ephesians 2:14-22!

(3.) What is the end result of bitterness, hatred, and other things that are not of God? (Prov. 14:10; Acts 8:23; Rom. 3:14; Eph. 4:31; Heb. 12:15)

(4.) But what are the end results of forgiveness and reconciliation? And what other things might Holy Scripture teach us about these things? (Gen. 33:4 AND 50:15-21; Luke 15: (ALL!) AND 11:1-4; Matt. 18:21-35; Eph. 4:17-32; Col. 3:12-14)

HOMEWORK: Find someone that may have wronged you that you see everyday and take the time to implement the steps suggested here. Then, if possible, go the extra mile if necessary to make things right with that individual. YOU TAKE THE INITIATIVE THIS WEEK TO FORGIVE! Also, go through this same process with someone else in your past who might not be present with you right now that caused you great damage and harm. Go to God on their behalf and intercede for them. Then write down what changes took place after you have done this assignment NOT ONLY in your own life, but in the lives of others during the rest of the week.

UNIT III, LESSON 4: Play The Deguello At The Point Of NO Return

The unit that we are in right now is highly focused on what it takes to travel the road back home to recovery. But there's a major stumbling block on this road--and that is indecision and the unwillingness to make the necessary decision to change into new patterns and methods of thinking. And as your guide through this Siberia, I wish to HIGHLY warn you that this stumbling block is one of the most dangerous in nature. IF you fail to use the right methods in removing this stumbling block...or worse, decide to turn back from here and go back where you started--then one thing will be for certain...you will NEVER be able to leave Siberia unless and until you learn to do so. And I REFUSE to be responsible for what happens to you next should you succumb to cowardice.

In case you haven't already noticed it by now, Siberia is NOT for cowards or those who wish to take the easy route through life pampered and spoiled with dreams of butlers and servants delicately catering to your every whim and need. In fact, Siberia is a pretty rough country to go through. Note here that I said go THROUGH--not just spectate or visit. The place has many dangers and snares that we must avoid if we are to survive here. On top of this we are also forced to fight a war the likes of which even I have not had to fight during my own time here.

As the Apostle Paul said to the Ephesians, "Finally, be strong in the Lord and in his mighty power. Put on the full armor of God so that you can take your stand against the devil's schemes. For our struggle is not against flesh and blood, but against the rulers, against the authorities, against the powers of this dark world and against the spiritual forces of evil in the heavenly realms. Therefore put on the full armor of God, so that when the day of evil comes, you may be able to stand your ground, and after you have done everything, to stand. Stand firm, then with the belt of truth buckled around your waist, with the breastplate of righteousness in place, and with your feet fitted with readiness that comes from the gospel of peace. In addition to all this, take up the shield of faith, with which you can extinguish all the flaming arrows of the evil one. Take the helmet of salvation and the sword of the Spirit, which is the word of God. And pray in the Spirit on all occasions with all kinds of prayers and requests..." (Eph. 6:10-18)

You see, it takes a lot to get through this place called Siberia. But one thing that you CANNOT have as you travel on through this harsh land is indecision. James 1:5-8 adds, "If any of you lacks wisdom, he should ask God, who gives generously to all without finding fault, and it will be given to him. But when he asks, he must believe and not doubt, because he who doubts is like a wave of the sea, blown and tossed by the wind. That man should not think he will receive anything from the Lord; he is a double-minded man, unstable in all he does."

In some places, you might be able to get by with this indecision thing--but here in Siberia, ANY small trace of indecision can be instantly fatal to you. If you are not determined enough to decide NOW where you will go from here AND STICK TO IT, the chances are very good that you will not survive even the next winter that is sure to come your way here. In some places, indecision won't hurt you--but in Siberia, if you are not even sure of the very next step to take from here, then YOU WILL CERTAINLY fall of the ledge to your death.

Even now, we come to the fork in the road--and here comes one last decision that you MUST make! Oh, hurry--choose wisely and smartly now BEFORE IT'S TOO LATE! One choice leads to life--the other leads to death. WHICH ONE WILL YOU CHOOSE? QUICKLY NOW--you CANNOT put this off. You cannot afford to be indecisive and unstable here. The choice is between life or death, freedom or bondage, blessing or curses--AND THERE IS NO MIDDLE GROUND OR FENCESTRADDLING ALLOWED!! Hurry up--MAKE YOUR CHOICE!!!

God says to you the same thing he said to the Israelites: "See, I set before you today life and prosperity, death and destruction. For I command you today to love the Lord your God, to walk in His ways, and to keep His commands, decrees, and laws; then you will live and increase, and the Lord your God will bless you in the land you are entering to possess. But if your heart turns away and you are not obedient, and if you are drawn away to bow down to other gods and worship them, I declare to you this day that you will certainly be destroyed. You will not live long in the land you are crossing the Jordan to enter and possess.

"This day I call heaven and earth as witnesses against you that I have set before you life and death, blessings and curses. Now choose life, so that you and your children may live and that you may love the Lord your God, listen to his voice, and hold fast to him. For the Lord is your life, and he will give you many years in the land he swore to give to your fathers, Abraham, Isaac, and Jacob." (Deut. 30:15-20)

In the closing part of Act II of "Phantom of the Opera", the Phantom urges Christine to make a decision once and for all whether or not she will formally decide to stay with him for the rest of her life:

"...Past the point of no return
The final threshold

The games we've played 'til now are at an end
Past the thought of if or when
No use resisting
Abandon thought and let the dream descend
What raging fire shall fill the soul
What rich desire unlocked since borne
What sweet seduction lies before us?
Past the point of no return
The final threshold
What woman's guarded secrets will be learned
Beyond the point of no return."

Here in Siberia, this is the place of which the locals like to call here "The Point of No Return". When outsiders come to this fork, the locals notice something interesting about the outsiders who come here--these folks will usually never come back to this exact same spot again. Those rare souls that by the slightest chance do are never the same one way or another after they come to this point in the journey and never choose the same path twice. If you'll notice something about this place, you'll find something else even more fascinating about "The Point of No Return" (or "the Point", as we will from here refer to it). If you keep going straight (which no one in their right mind would want to do), notice the next place you end up--a dead end that leads to a fatal descent into the valley below.

Now take a quick look at the contrasting width of the two roads. The one here on the right is called the "Narrow Road" because the road is extremely narrow most of the way with room enough to fit in about one person at a time. It's also a one-way road that has a lot of curves and treacherous climbs within it full of danger. But years ago in history, a hearty band of pioneering travelers found an interesting archeological find that lets us know where the final stop on this road is--the city of FREEDOM that lies right on the border and that is THE key to anyone's release from this Siberian prison. Past reports that I have received from those who stayed on this road and have never strayed from it have found themselves--full of freedom, happiness, and abundant life with joy unspeakable. The number of people that have found their freedom by going down this road has been only a handful--but I can sure tell you that these people are a lot of fun to be around. Some of them are my closest friends and my biggest supporters who contribute and stand behind why I try to do what I do for you here in Siberia. Without them, you wouldn't be able to have the proper information necessary to choose the right path here at "the Point".

But what saddens me and breaks my heart most is seeing those who decide to take the path on the left and the final end of those who do. You will notice the name of this path as the "Broad Interstate Highway". It looks nice; it's paved and smooth--in short, a lot of people love to travel down this highway. People cruise up and down this multi-lane highway and even have a great number of outdoor picnics and barbeques and seem to have a lot of fun here.

But the locals here have an interesting nickname for this road: "The Highway of Destruction". Why? Because both they and I know where this interstate highway leads to: death and destruction. You know the Siberian prison that you've been in? Well, guess where this road leads back to? It leads you right back where you started from--the main prison unit itself. And the even sadder part about it is this--most who take this highway back to the prison are never seen or heard from ever again. Rumors are that those who dared to escape from that prison, but then come here to "the Point" and decide to take the "Broad Interstate Highway" and then subsequently find themselves back in prison are treated even worse by the Adversary and his guards than before their escape. People are then summarily tortured, maimed, or even--bleep forbid--KILLED--and no one ever hears from them again.

"The Point" makes this statement from the Savior a poignant and somber reminder of the seriousness of the decision of the choice of path taken from here: "Enter through the narrow gate. For wide is the gate and broad is the road that leads to destruction, and many enter through it. But small is the gate and narrow the road that leads to life, and only a few find it." (Matt. 6:25) If you stay in indecision and uncertainty here at "the Point", you will either fall off the ledge, stall in inactivity, or worse--go backwards in your journey here. If you take the "Narrow Road", the road WILL be rough and rocky; but the things you will see at the end of the trip will definitely be worth the effort and exertion it took to travel that road. If you decide, though, to go down the "Broad Interstate", you might be happy for a season, but the end of the road will cost you more than you have got.

But the locals also say that there is something else you should do before you start down one road or another. There's a local custom that I would highly recommend that you follow that makes good sense. The locals believe that anyone who keeps this tradition will see prosperity and good success on their journey on whatever road you decide to take.

The tradition originates from a story that occurred around the time that Texas was trying to gain their independence from Mexico. The 6,000 troops of Santa Anna surrounded the mission of the Alamo where just under 200 Texans were held up in with no realistic hope of reinforcements. Legend has it that Santa Anna, prior to the battle of the Alamo, ordered his bugler to play a tune called the "Deguello". When Santa Anna gave this order, he was, in a sense, telling the Texans in military terms the following: that no quarter (in otherwords, NO MERCY) would be given to the Texans, no prisoners would be taken (in otherwords, ANYONE captured would be IMMEDIATELY shot on the spot), AND nothing less than total and unconditional surrender by the Texans would be accepted by Santa Anna. The translation for the Texans--NONE would make it out alive if the Mexicans had their way.

The locals, though, say something else about the people they see at "the Point" that follow this custom. They have said numerous times to me through stories and firsthand eyewitness accounts which they claim gives even further proof to the story of travelers who wind up here at the Point. How can the natives tell exactly which road someone will probably go? It is usually by the direction the traveler blows the horn towards. If a traveler blows the horn towards the "Narrow Road", they most likely will eventually go in that direction. They also warn me that if you blow the horn towards the "Broad Interstate" not to be surprised if later on you're bound to wind up dead on the side of the road over there. And something else of a spiritual nature becomes apparent to the locals--one of the ways is that which Satan urges us to go on and the other is where God passionately pleads for you to go. I can't confirm or deny any of these rumors--but I've personally seen and heard enough here to make me very careful of which road and which choices I might decide to take. I would highly advise that you follow suit.

We'll use the DISCUSSION QUESTIONS this time as a combination road map and supply checklist that might make the difference in deciding what the best choice for you might be and to take whatever the best road from here might be to where you want to go next.

[DISCUSSION QUESTIONS:]

(1.) What does Peter, the one whom Christ said would be "...t he Rock on which I will build my Church", advise us to do? What does He want us to have? (2 Pet. 1:5-9)

_____

(2.) (v. 11) Why, according to Peter, should we have those things? _____

(3.) Now let's look at each of these qualities a little bit in depth. What does the Word say in particular about each of these? As you do this, also don't forget to define each of these terms as well while you're at it:

(a.) Goodness _____

(b.) Knowledge/wisdom? _____

(c,) Self-control? _____

(d.) Perserverance? _____
(e.) Godliness? _____

(f.) Brotherly kindness? _____

(g.) Love? _____

[I think this time, though, that I want YOU to look up these things up in your own Bible with a good concordance to help you out so that you can start to learn to study the Word for yourself!]

(4.) What is important about the qualities listed in (#3.)? Why does God think that we are all such in desperate need for them? _____

(5.) What did the Rav Shaul urge the Colossians to do? (Col. 3:1-17) _____

(6.) Now let's check and see a little bit about determination and making a right and proper decision on what to do next. What did the prophet Isaiah say that he had resolve to do? (Isa. 50:7) _____

(7.) What might be some things that you should determine to do? (1 Cor. 15:58; Deut. 4:9; Phil. 3:14)

_____

(8.) Now how does wisdom enter the picture? What role should it play in the choices you make? (Phil. 1:9; 2 Tim. 2:7; Ps. 25:4; 27:11; 90:12; 119:12, 18, 34, & 125; James 1:3)

(9.) The book of Proverbs in particular has a lot to say about wisdom. What do you notice about the following verses? (Proverbs 1:2, 7, & 20; 2:2 & 6-10; 3:13; 4:3-7; 5:1; 7:4; 8:3; 9:1 & 12-14; 10:13 & 23) (This is just to name a few.)

[(Note:) Try this for a good exercise while you're here in Proverbs. Count how many times this book says something about wisdom and, at the same time, see of those references how many of them also relate in some way to decisionmaking.]

(10.) Now how about perserverance? What might God's Word say about this? (Heb. 3:14; Gal. 3:9; 2 Thess. 3:13; 2 Tim. 2:3; John 10:28 & 29; 1 John 5:13; 2 Tim. 1:13; 1 Thess. 5:21; Heb. 10:23; John 17:11 & 12; 2 Tim. 4:18; Rom. 8:38 & 39; 2 Tim. 3:15; Heb. 12:1; 2 Cor. 1:21; Eph. 6:13; Col. 1:23; 1 Cor. 16:13)

(11.) What in particular might patience and perserverance add to our lives? (Prov. 14:29 & 19:11; 2 Cor. 1:6 & 6:4; 2 Pet. 1:6; Rev. 1:9)

(12.) But you CANNOT do anything else BEFORE you do something that God considers EXTREMELY vital and crucial! What might that be? (James 4:7-10)

[(Special Note:) Check out how the New World Dictionary of the American Language defines the word "surrender":

"...(1.) to give up possession of or power over; yield to another on demand or compulsion; (2.) to give up claim to; give over or yield, especially voluntarily, as in favor of another; (3.) to give up or abandon [surrendering all hope]

(4.) to yield or resign (oneself) to an emotion, influence, etc.; -vi. (1.) to give oneself up to another's power or control, especially as a prisoner; (2.) to give in [to something]; yield; to surrender to temptation, a whim, etc."]

God seems to want to tell you here at "the Point" that there are several choices you MUST make right now that will determine what your future destiny will be. If you make the WRONG choices now, you will be soon going on the road to destruction-- the "Broad Interstate" if you will. If you make the RIGHT choices now, though, God will personally see to it that you will be able to prosper and live and declare the works of the Lord. And what does it all involve here? This will deal with the SPECIFIC things that you decide that you will decide to surrender to. Here's the questions I feel you should ask yourself:

WHICH OF THE FOLLOWING ARE YOU GOING TO MAKE AN ACTIVE, CONSCIOUS DECISION TO SURRENDER TO? (YOU CAN'T HAVE BOTH-- YOU CAN ONLY HAVE ONE OR THE OTHER!!)

(1.) Fear of the uncertainty that lies ahead OR COMPLETE trust in Him to see you through the trials you face?
(2.) The shackles of the past that have bound you OR the freedom in Christ that awaits you?
(3.) Those fickle opinions or statements that man might say OR the eternal, everliving, never-changing Word of God and what it has to say for YOUR life?
(4.) Doubt and fear OR faith, love, devotion, trust, and confidence in Him?
(5.) The circumstances around you that say, "YOU CAN'T!" OR our God who says, "YOU CAN!!"?

[BUT MOST IMPORTANTLY....]
(6.) The ways of this world and the Adversary--OR the divinely ordained and ordered steps of the ways of God?

You see, what you decide to surrender TO will eventually lead you in what you will eventually BECOME! So don't be surprised if where you say you will wind up is where you do eventually end up. You need to make the choices NOW on what you will surrender to so that later on when trials and tribulations come that you will not surrender to the wrong thing. You are going to surrender to something eventually--why not surrender to the RIGHT things? IT'S NOT the fact that you have decided to surrender to something in the first place that counts--what should matter instead is the thing that you surrender TO! Are you going to resign life and give up all hope OR will you surrender to the God of ALL hope? IT'S YOUR CHOICE!!

Oh--something else I forgot to tell you about Santa Anna and the Texans and the final outcome of it all...when the "Deguello" was played, the Texans might have lost that particular battle--BUT THEY DID NOT LOSE THE WAR AND THEY DID NOT SURRENDER! And if that doesn't take the cake, check this out...it was Santa Anna himself that would be eventually forced to surrender to the Texans and go back home to Mexico City in disgrace. But just as there can be NO San Jacinto without an Alamo and no Approtomox without a Fort Sumter, so it is here at "the Point" that you cannot have a release from your Siberian prison until you have made an ACTIVE, CONSCIOUS decision to surrender to something bigger than yourself. That which you surrender to will be what you eventually serve. It's time to make the right choice! It's time to "play the Deguello" at the Point of No Return and point it in the exact direction you wish to head from here. For the choice and the direction you point to and the things that you will decide to surrender to and serve will literally make the difference between life or death.

[HOMEWORK:] So what choice will YOU make at "The Point of No Return"? Answer the questions I just alluded to about surrendering and CHOOSE YE THIS DAY WHO YOU WILL SURRENDER TO AND SERVE! Then, act appropriately according to the choices you've just made.

[PRAYER;] Creator Father, Lord God Almighty, and Lord Jesus/Y'shua:

I'm here now at this "point of no return" and know now that I MUST make a quality choice about the rest of my life from here. And I choose this day to surrender ONLY to YOU, Your ways, Your purposes, and Your good plan for my life. I REFUSE to surrender to those things the world and Your adversary would like for me to do. I REFUSE to surrender AT ALL to the bondages and hindrances of the past, the pressures of the present, or the uncertainties and fears of the future. But instead, I lay them down at Your feet and surrender these and everything else I have ONLY to

You. And I will trust You, obey You, love You, and serve You ONLY as a (man/woman) that's consecrated, separated, and totally surrendered ONLY to You and You alone. And I say this in the name of Your Son who surrendered His own life for me--Y'shua Ha'Meshiach/the Lord Jesus Christ--AMEN!!!!

UNIT III, LESSON 5: True Religion Undefiled--Pray For Those Who Persecute You

I know that what I am about to write here might upset a few apple carts, but maybe sometimes that IS the exact thing that needs to be done in order to see that you become what I know our God would truly like for you to be. Just as important to me here in writing this in seeing that YOU recover from what you and/or others may have afflicted upon yourself is the desire that I have to work on insuring that the damage the Adversary has caused on all of us is NOT ONLY repaired, but turned back squarely on his head where it truly belongs in the first place.

Maybe I can use my past experience as a Grand Juror as well as prison ministry to help further shed a little more light on this. In some of the various times I have went into the units, it was always remarkable to me the number of men I have seen with absolutely downcast faces without much hope or joy on them. But what shocked me more about this was when in the grand jury room I might see a prisoner testifying in front of us begging and pleading to let him off, give him one more chance, and that he was truly sorry for his actions--blah, blah, blah. All of this while at the time JUST BEFORE we might hear that prisoner give his testimony we heard from a police officer who usually gave VERY credible evidence that the same prisoner who seemed repentant and who would naturally try to show a good face to us all the while wearing an orange county jail jumpsuit was caught recklessly driving at speeds down the middle of a city street that would even make most truckers on the interstate nervous and with breath test results that shot through and went past the allowable legal limits (and in which the officers usually, more times than not, were VERY conscientious and meticulous about the manner they did their jobs and the procedures and policies they were required to follow in carrying out their duties).

In contrast, I might notice whenever some of the victims of these same crimes would testify before us that usually one of three things might happen: EITHER they were so scared to death of testifying for one reason or another due to a possible perceived threat of retaliation by the offender or other unknown fears that they actually begged and pleaded for us to let the offender go and pretend that it was nothing (even though the District Attorney was insistent for various reasons on prosecuting the case) OR they were actually trying to cover something up and hide the fact that they had committed a crime themselves and were trying to pin the blame on someone else OR that they were so mad and bitter at the alleged criminal that they wanted to throw the book at him/her and that he/she was the scum of the earth and wasn't even fit to live as a human being.

Have you ever watched various police shows or courtroom dramas on TV in the past and observed those things? What is the average picture they might paint of the offender? What about that of the victim? Might the offender usually be portrayed as conniving, manipulative, and anxious to do whatever it takes to avoid getting into trouble or prison or whatever unpleasant fate might await them? Could the victim, in contrast, be easily portrayed as helpless, defenseless, grief-stricken, embittered, and angry at the criminal? What stereotypical images does our world usually present of these folks?

But now, I think I wonder some even deeper questions on this. WHAT ABOUT WHAT OUR SAVIOR REALLY WANTS FOR US??? What would HE like to see from both of these groups? Does He in all reality think the victim has spiritual justifications for what has happened and for acting in the way that he/she does towards the one that committed the crime against them?

Before I start beginning to tread on what is possibly some very dangerous ground and trampling over things in the natural that I shouldn't, I need to first emphasize the following: I DO NOT necessarily say that the legal system should not be used as an appropriate recourse to handle all grievances and that we should never allow the State to punish those guilty of criminal or civil acts. BLEEP FORBID that we should do that. I DO NOT necessarily say that criminals should not be held accountable for their actions. TO THE CONTRARY, even the Apostle Paul addressed this when he told the Romans:

"...Everyone must submit himself to the governing authorities, for there is no authority except that which God has established. The authorities that exist have been established by God. Consequently, he who rebels against the authority is rebelling against what God has instituted, and those who do so will bring judgment on themselves. For rulers hold no terror for those who do right, but for those who do wrong. Do you want to be free from fear of the one in authority? Then do what is right and he will commend you. For he is God's servant to do you good. But if you do wrong, be afraid, for he does not bear the sword for nothing. He is God's servant, an agent of wrath to bring punishment on the wrongdoer. Therefore, it is necessary to submit to the authorities, not only because of possible punishment but also because of conscience.
"...This is also why you pay taxes, for the authorities are God's servants, who give their full time to governing. Give everyone what you owe him: if you owe taxes, pay taxes; if revenue, then revenue; if respect, then respect; if honor, then honor." (Rom. 13:1-7)

But let's face it: what happens AFTER the trial is over with, the judge has given the verdict, the criminal is then sent to prison for who knows however long (or even possibly sentenced to death in some cases), and the victim is given what is thought to be justice and due compensation for damages caused by the offender.

PROBLEM--usually the victim IS NOT TRULY allowed to say his/her mind AT ALL until it is too late in the process and the offender is NOT allowed to be directly confronted by the victim with the consequences of their actions. And to add insult to injury and make matters worse before our God, the mere thought of the possibility of reconciliation and forgiveness between BOTH affected parties IS NOT EVEN TOLERATED OR ALLOWED--the exact VERY SAME thing that might actually bind up and heal the wounds in between them and that might possibly turn what was once a tragedy into a potential triumph. (Is all of this making some form of sense and convicting you in your spirit RIGHT NOW? Are you beginning to detect that something here is truly fishy in Denmark?)

Some people as I write this are just now beginning to talk about a concept called "restorative justice" here in the state that I currently live in. There is one problem with that concept, though, in a way--THE RESTORATION OF ANYTHING CANNOT REALISTICALLY BEGIN UNLESS THE PROCESS OF RECONCILIATION IS ALLOWED TO BEGIN AND THEN BE PLANTED, NOURISHED AND CHERISHED!! No true wounds or barriers between the parties can EVER be truly healed unless or until both parties have a chance to walk in each other's moccasins a while, see that there is a need to reconcile with the other party, and then TAKE GODLY ACTIONS towards that eventual and essential first goal. IN OTHERWORDS--NOTHING can be restored until it is first brought back to the original starting place and ALL past unresolved issues are taken care of!! (Talk about a process that is HARD to do...)

Our God is now beginning to thunder down some things to us about this. You see, reconciliation IS HIS VERY HEART!! For instance, without true repentance from our sins, reconciliation with Him in a CLOSE and INTIMATE relationship, and restoration to a BETTER place than where we used to be spiritually, WE ARE ETERNALLY DOOMED!! The same principles hold true in any of these crimes (ESPECIALLY in the particular subject areas that we are focusing in during this particular study.)

In some cases, face-to-face reconciliation is not advised and not appropriate--but in general, those situations are usually the exception rather than God's accepted rules. WHY IS THIS SO? Because the God that I serve DOES NOT feel that never-ending separation, hostility, bitterness, and anger is His ultimate best for you! AU CONTRARE--3rd John 2 says, "Dear friend, I pray that you may enjoy good health and that all may go well with you, even as your soul is getting along well." He truly desires for all to be RECONCILED!!! (2 Cor. 5:18-20) If you might look closely in a good concordance, you will find something interesting here about this word called reconciliation. Various forms of this word appear at least eight times in the Old Testament and thirteen times in the New Testament. Of the majority of those references, most of the time they will either deal with the need to reconcile with the Father Himself OR with the need to reconcile with our brother or sister. And it will usually furthermore equate our reconciliation with each other to our current state of relationship with our God.

But I can sense you asking me this: "Yeah, right...But who is my brother/sister/neighbor?" And I wouldn't be surprised if you also decided to ask the same question Cain did after he killed Abel: "Am I my brother's keeper?" Well, why don't you look for yourself at Luke 10:25-37 real quickly and see and decide for yourself what it says your brother or neighbor truly is? Then see what Keener says about various parts of this passage here:

> "...Jewish teachers usually used "neighbor" to mean
> "fellow Israelite". Leviticus 19:18 clearly means "fellow
> Israelite" in the immediate context, but the less immediate
> context applies the principle also to any non-Israelite in
> the land...Jesus' questioner would hate Samaritans, yet he is
> forced to follow the moral example of a Samaritan in Jesus'
> story. This parable forced him to answer his own question,
> "Who is my neighbor?"" (Keener, pp. 217 & 218)

Powerful stuff, eh? But that's not the end of what He has to say by any means. I think there is a much more fundamental point to this that can be easily given by the Apostle James that leads to an even more central point I wish to make--"Religion that God our Father accepts as pure and faultless is this: to look after orphans and widows in their distress and to keep oneself from being polluted by the world." WHAT SHOULD OUR FOCUS BE IN REGARDS TO THIS PASSAGE? AND--MOST IMPORTANTLY--WHAT MIGHT BE (in my very limited opinion) the biggest things one might need to do to keep the process of recovery from your current situation be?

Simple--to stop focusing on ourselves and those things that have held us back for so long and to instead on those things our God wants us to focus on. Or to put it another way--YOU turn away from trying to take care of your own business and instead give it to God and ask HIM to fix it. THEN--you instead start to focus on going about in His strength and power and doing the business that HE wants YOU to do for Him. THEN--when you take care of His business, He will then begin to take care of yours. As the Savior said Himself: "Whatever you sow, that you shall also reap." When you take your focus of your circumstances and instead place that same focus right square on Him, the circumstances will pale in comparison to the mightiness of the God that we serve.

I remember a situation where I was assisting someone with teaching a Promise Keepers class at one of the state prison units close to where I live. At that time, I was again facing the possibility of eviction from my apartment. Let me tell you something about eviction--whenever you know that you do not have the money to pay your landlord what is due them and you dread the knock on the door or even a notice in the mail or whatever, believe me--you will do everything in your power to avoid seeing him or her if at all possible.

It was interesting one time that after I had went with the man that I was assisting at the time had finished one night in the unit that I had one of the weirdest thoughts in my life. It was as if I were actually wanting to be in that unit instead of them so that I could avoid the heavy pressures and responsibilities that were upon me at the time. I even commented about this to the man I was helping and we even talked about it a bit. Man, was that thought really tempting to me.

But then, I came back to my senses when I thought about what these prisoners went through in the units. I might appreciate the financial security and freedom from responsibility, but I would be forced to trade it for what amounts to be virtual slavery to an equally unforgiving and unrelenting system that shows no mercy and places extremely strict demands upon those within its confines. But even then, my God was teaching me about the importance of the fact that when you only focus on the problem and the circumstances around you, THAT IS ALL YOU WILL BE ABLE TO SEE!! But when you take your eyes off the circumstances and instead do what God asks that you do for others, you will in turn be very blessed in what you do. And on top of it, the Adversary receives from us a very big black eye and a major defeat as a result.

But what is this thing about "...true religion undefiled"? And how in His holy name could this be done even in the worst circumstances? I think that I might be bold enough to say the following in response:

(1.) WALK A MILE IN SOMEONE ELSE'S MOCCASINS!!--Remember what I said earlier in this book about trying to see things from the other's point of view? Well, this becomes absolutely crucial here.

Prisoners--have you ever dared to imagine and think about problems that you might have had a direct part in causing that the victim now has to live and deal with for the rest of their lives? Can you even grasp the pain and grief that you might have needlessly caused them either by your recklessness or even by your deliberate (or even possibly unplanned, spur-of-the-moment) schemes)? What about the consequences of YOUR actions that THEY have to now pay for as a result--of severe financial ruin, physical/emotional/mental/psychological problems, or even possibly worse--DEATH of a spouse or a loved one? THINK ABOUT IT HARD!! Did you even consider SOMEONE ELSE'S desires and needs of your own BEFORE you went and did what you did? And has all of this TRULY forced you to work towards making PERMANENT, LASTING, POSITIVE changes in your own life as a result?

Victims--have you ever seen things from the prisoner's perspective? Are you even aware that at one time before the incident occurred that this criminal may have once been victimized himself/herself? Do you now see the absolute hopelessness, desperation, and frustration they now truly feel about being in a hole that they themselves can't get out of in their own effort? Do you realize that the odds for an ex-con being able to simply get a decent job after release or sometimes even harder for them as it is for you in your own job search? And do you even realize that if they may have not been able to grow up emotionally to start out with due to their past background and upbringing that they will have a harder time to dealing with life and reality in general both before and after their release?

   If BOTH groups would think about the needs of the other and concern themselves with what our God desires for them to think about INSTEAD of being mired in self-centeredness, who knows how much more our God would bless them as they do it?

******(2.) TRUE RELIGION UNDEFILED==PRAY FOR THOSE WHO PERSECUTE YOU

I know that now you're probably sitting at the edge of your seat and shouting to me, "WHAT???? PRAY FOR THEM!! NEVER!!!!" But there's a funny thing that I've noticed about God's usual modus operandi (for those of you that don't speak Latin, you can roughly translate that to "methods of operation")--it is EXACTLY BACKWARDS AND OPPOSITE of the way we as humans might tend to naturally do things.

Think of it this way--when we zig, God might usually instead zag. If we might get angry at something, God in contrast might usually decide to instead be merciful to them and give them a break. But also--when we think that something is right, sometimes God will tend to think that it is abhorrent to His nostrils. And sometimes the things that we think will bring honor and glory unto Him will in His eyes be worth no more than filthy rags. The prophet Isaiah might have something to add here on this: "Seek the Lord while he may be found; call on him while he is near. Let the wicked forsake his way and the evil man his thoughts. Let him turn to the LORD, and he will have mercy on him, and to our God, for he will freely pardon. For my thoughts are not your thoughts, neither are my ways your ways my ways," declares the LORD. As the heavens are higher than the earth, so are my ways higher than your ways and my thoughts than your thoughts." (Isaiah 55:6-9)

And what might one of HIS thoughts be for part of what He might feel be the best method of your recovery? Our Savior roars back with his Sermon on the Mount response: "...You have heard that it was said, 'Love your neighbor and hate your enemy.' But I tell you: Love your enemies and pray for those who persecute you, that you may be sons of your Father in heaven. He cause his sun to rise on the evil and the good, and sends rain on the righteous and the unrighteous. If you love those who love you, what reward will you get? Are not even the tax collectors doing that? And if you greet only your brothers, what are you doing more than others? Do not even pagans do that? Be perfect, therefore, as your heavenly Father is perfect." (Matt. 5: 43-48)

Our Savior adds later on in that famous sermon: "Do not judge, or you too will be judged. For in the same way you judge others, you will be judged, and with the measure you use, it will be measured to you. Why do you look at the speck of sawdust in your brother's eye and pay no attention to the plank in your own eye? How can you say to your brother, 'Let me take the speck out of your eye,' when all the time there is a plank in your own eye? You hypocrite, first take the plank out of your own eye, and then you will see clearly to remove the speck from your brother's eye."

Remember--when we zig, our God zags. When we tend to want to blow our top and want to give someone a piece of our mind, that's probably the exact time where God instead would desire that we be at our most merciful to others and their shortcomings. When we have nothing but hatred for someone else, the Savior wants us to pray and intercede for them instead. But it's NOT for the reasons that you might suspect- -NO!! It's NOT so that others can walk all over us as doormats--but so that

YOU can be blessed in the doing of that act and that our God can be much more freer to show his love and mercy to the other person, too.

(3.) BUT DON'T JUST PRAY FOR THEM!! ALSO TAKE ADVANTAGES OF OPPORTUNITIES YOU MIGHT HAVE TO SHOW THE MERCY THAT GOD WOULD HAVE FOR THEM!! Yes, I know--that is COMPLETELY illogical and definitely something only a "crazy" person would do. But then God DOES NOT always operate in the logical or in ways that we can easily grasp or conceive. Hey, He IS the Creator of the Universe--and He DOES have the absolute right to operate in the way that He would desire. He DOES NOT guarantee that you will be free from pain--but He HAS provided you with the way to escape from it and bear it. Therefore, doesn't it also stand to reason that He might also wish to do a similar thing for some other person on the planet--possibly to even the very one who caused you so much heartache and pain? God does specialize, you know, in turning what was evil into what will be to your eventual good.

Might it be possible that God might desire to turn the situation around by YOU taking a small part in the salvation, healing, and deliverance of the other party so that YOU can recover from your trauma? If we just might consider getting out of yourself and instead focusing on those things my God would have you do, who knows how much more could be done for all parties concerned? Could it be that through your mercy to the offending party that their life could be touched in a special, unique way not possible otherwise AND that, as a result, your own healing from the emotional, physical, and other problems that are the by-product of the hideous act that was committed unto you? I don't know honestly what to think about this personally--but this might be something that you might have to decide for yourself if this might be a valid path for you personally to take.

But how might one wish to follow through in showing mercy to someone? Mark Ensign comes back again with a thought or two on that from Exodus 20:20-26:

"There are four groups of people mentioned in Parsha Mishpatim: the stranger, the widow, the orphan, and the poor. There is a common denominator in this group--they are all without an advocate or a protector. The people that were in these catagories could easily be overlooked or taken advantage of. As we study Torah, we find that G-d himself took up their cause and is their advocate and protector. Here's what the L-rd says about these people:

"For the L-ord your G-d is...a mighty G-d...which regards not persons. He executes judgment of the fatherless

140

and widow, and loves the stranger...love therefore the stranger: for you were strangers in the land of Egypt." [Deverim (Deuteronomy) 10:17-19].

"...G-d tells us his heart; he does not regard persons. He shows no partiality. And then he reminds us of who we are--those who were once strangers, whom he delivered out of Egypt. In remembering who we are, we are then to turn and love the stranger. A widow was a woman who had lost her male protector and her source of financial support. She was put under the protection of the community. Once every three years, in addition to the regular gleanings of the annual harvest, a tithe of the harvest was shared with the widows, orphans, Levites, and strangers [Deuteronomy 14:28, 29; 26:12, 13). Can you imagine the peace that widows or orphans would experience within a community such as this? They would also be free to serve the L-rd and not have to struggle for their daily survival.

"Emulating our Father, we too must not be respecters of persons. We are to protect those who are without protection and assist those to whom we can minister as the servants of our Father. As Rav Shaul [the Apostle Paul) wrote to the believers in Rome, "For the passage quoted says that everyone who rest his trust on him will not be humiliated. (12) That means that there is no difference between Jew and Gentile...Adonai is the same for everyone, rich toward everyone who calls on him, (13) since everyone who calls on the name of Adonai will be delivered." [Romans 10:11-13]

"And he added in Galatians 3:26-29: "For in union with the Messiah, you are all children of G-d through this trusting faithfulness; (27) because as many of you as were immersed into the Messiah have clothed yourselves with the Messiah, in whom (28) there is neither Jew or Gentile, neither slave nor freeman, neither male nor female; for in union with the Messiah Y'shua, you are all one. (23) Also if you belong to the Messiah, you are the seed of Avraham and heirs according to the promise..."

Okay, but HOW could I go about turning what the Adversary meant for harm into good? Simple--INSTEAD OF CURSING THEM, BLESS THEM!! If the one that has offended you is in need, then do a little something to see that need is taken care of somehow. But in what ways could it be done? Ensign has a little something further to add to this discussion by his description of what he calls the "Eight Levels of Tzedekah (Charity)":

"Here are eight degrees or levels or tzedekah (charity)

on an ascending scale:

"The eighth and lowest level of charity is when one gives
charity grudgingly.
"The seventh level is when one gives less than he should,
but does so cheerfully.
"The sixth level is when one gives directly to the poor
upon being asked.
"The fifth level is when one gives the alms directly to
the poor without being asked.
"The fourth level is when the giving is indirect. The
recipient knows who the giver is, but the giver does not know
the identity of the recipient.
"The third level is when the giver knows the identity of
the recipient, but the recipient does not know the identity
of the giver.
"The second highest level is when the one who gives is
unaware of the recipient, who in turn is unaware of the
giver. (e.g., contributing to a charity fund)
"The highest form of charity is to help sustain a person
before he becomes impoverished, by offering a substantial
gift in a dignified manner or by extending a suitable loan,
or by helping him find employment or establish him in some
business so as to make it unnecessary for him to become
dependent on others."

And to top it all off, our Savior did say Himself: "Blessed are the merciful, for they
will be shown mercy." (Matt. 5:7) Isn't it only fair to our God that we be willing to
even show mercy (within reason, of course) and forgiveness to the one who offended
you? Isn't it only right and proper that we remain willing to extend mercy and
forgiveness to even those who have trespassed against us. If we do our part in this
end, God is then free to deal with the offender in His mercy INSTEAD of judgment
and can truly change a stony heart into one of flesh.

(4.) TAKE ACTIVE STEPS TO RECONCILE WITH THE OTHER PARTY IF AT
ALL POSSIBLE!!

Why do I keep harping on this? It is again because our natural tendency is to seek
vengeance and try to get our rightful piece of flesh. But it does NOT make the heart
of our God truly glad and in peace with you. The Adversary wishes to ONLY steal,

kill, destroy, tear apart, and break things. But our God--MY GOD--desires to mend, heal, repair, restore, refresh, and renew us every day and to, more importantly, reconcile us with BOTH others AND Himself. Doesn't that sound much more wonderful and alive with realistic hope and possibility? It sure does to me--HOW ABOUT YOU???

But again--how can this be done? Maybe this would be an opportunity to have a final recap about all we just talked about here:

     (a.) Go through Lindsey Roberts' 2-Step Formula Prayer
 For Forgiveness (go back to Lesson 3 of this unit for details...)!
     (b.) PRAY for the well-being and concern for the condition of the party who offended you.
     (c.) Find a way to take care of the OTHER party's needs--AND NOT necessarily yours.
     (d.) TAKE THE INITIATIVE TO ACTIVELY FORGIVE AND RECONCILE IF POSSIBLE!!

The conclusion of this matter? I say that's INSTEAD of dwelling on the bad of this, let's instead use this as a spiritual weapon that we can push back at the Adversary and that will ultimately propel the Gospel of the Kingdom light years ahead of where it is now. And also, through praying for those who once persecuted and harmed you--turning what was a Shakespearean tragedy into a beautiful piece of music fit for our Master to perform for us. When the focus is on the right thing--our Savior and Lord--then we can live continually in victory despite the circumstances that buffet around us and be that special blessing to others in need of Him...even to those who once hated us without a cause. And our God can then be allowed to miraculously turn what was once bad into something that is for our ultimate well-being and good.

DISCUSSION QUESTIONS:

(1.) What have been some ways you were harmed in the past? How have you in particular been hurt?

(2.) What did you once feel about those who hurt you and how do you feel about them right now?

(3.) What are the enemies of ANY KIND that you are currently facing? What pressures and stresses are you now having to deal with in your current situation right now?

(4.) What might be some REALISTIC ways that you could still show mercy even to those who harmed you WITHOUT hurting yourself needlessly in the process?

PRAYER: Creator Father, Lord God Almighty, and Lord Jesus/Y'shua--Thank You for talking to me today about the need to do good to those who have harmed me in the past or who are causing great damage to my life right now. Help me to use today as a way to take advantage of opportunities to better serve You by NOT retaliating against my enemies--but instead to follow exactly what Your only Son said about "... praying for those who persecute you" and that we need to do good to those who have harmed us. And as we do these things today, I also ask that you would quickly and speedily heal all of those wounds that this person inflicted on me. And help me to turn these past defeats in joy. This I ask in the name of your Son--Y'shua Ha'Meshiach/the Lord Jesus Christ--AMEN!!

UNIT IV, LESSON I--A Time For War and A Time For Peace: The Process of Victim/Offender Reconciliation

This may be one of the most difficult chapters that I have ever had to write because I am not sure just how many have dared write in this way before--and also that this is even newer ground for even the most experienced veterans in the area of restorative justice ministry. But I feel that this revelation that I feel my God has started to impart to me on this will be an absolute blessing to you should the things said here be properly examined and applied in accordance to the Word of God.

I do not know why exactly it is, but I have at various times seemed almost drawn and compelled to look closely at the Old Testament book of Ecclesiates. In fact, this book in which most people will usually zoom by on the Biblical interstate to what they might otherwise perceive as more interesting things to me usually entices me so much that I cannot help but to pull off that interstate highway and stop in for an occasional visit from time to time. This book seems to almost describe best to me the conditions and futility of life in this physical world in a way that no other part of Scripture does.

For instance, look closely at chapter 3 of that book for a minute or two. I faintly recall a song that was released in the late 1960s by a group called the Byrds in which it EXACTLY fits word for word with the first part of this chapter. [I think the title is something like "To everything, turn, turn, turn" or something like that--I don't know. But if you're able to get a classic rock album of any kind at your nearby record store, chances are that this particular song will usually be included as one of the cuts on the album. Listen to this song--and I figure that you will know what it means after you hear it.]

There in this passage of Scripture is probably one of the best statements our God will give in regards to two things: one, the matter and nature of God's timing in how He relates to us as individuals; and two, more importantly--the very need for us to realize that sooner or later in God's timescale, a sort of reconciliation MUST occur of one kind or another (or otherwise--NO ONE will truly be satisfied or fulfilled IN ANY WAY). To us, we might consider going through this process of reconciliation (if we even decide to do it at all) as a luxury or something that we might consider doing if and only if it is convenient for us and doesn't cause ourselves too much pain.

BUT IN GOD'S EYES--it is NOT a matter of IF you should reconcile to the one who either hurt you or to whom you personally have hurt--IT IS WHEN!! I guess that I seem to think that God has an incessant demand and plea for us that EVERYTHING

AND EVERYONE must be reconciled and put back together to either the way it was before or (preferably) a BETTER place than it was before the unfortunate incident happened. As I have said in previous chapters, it is God's own heart and earnest desire that reconciliation and restoration take place where hurts and wounds still remain. IN FACT, our very Savior/Meshiach went so far as to make mention of this in the middle of the Sermon on the Mount in Matthew 5:23-26 when He said: "Therefore, if you are offering your gift at the altar and there remember that your brother has something against you, leave your gift there in front of the altar. First go and be reconciled to your brother; then come and offer your gift.

"Settle matters quickly with your adversary who is taking you to court. Do it while you are still with him on the way, or he may hand you over to the judge, and the judge may hand you over to the officer, and you may be thrown into prison. I tell you the truth, you will not get out until you have paid the last penny."

I know that the things I am about to say that follow will be VERY extremely hard words for all parties to take--but I fear that if I DON'T take the time to say them that I will not only disobey my God and the good calling that He has given me; but also will be doing everyone else a GREAT disservice in the process. To me, it just seems that our God values reconciliation a whole lot higher in honor and esteem than any offerings we give to any church or worthy cause. I have become convinced that if we gave our God ten million dollars a piece for a church building product and yet can't even muster the guts to face each other and formally resolve once and for all the issues that separate us--that the gift will smell like to God worse than the smell from a feed lot. Maybe instead of burying our money, we need to bury a few hatchets instead....this all coming, of course, from a God who tends to think that obedience is better than sacrifice.

In this lesson (that I believe will be a turning point in your life not only in these studies that you have been engaged in so far), I therefore feel that it is way past time to urge both the victim and the offender to do something EXTREMELY radical that will do the Adversary of our God great and major damage. It will be, by far, the hardest thing you have ever done in your life so far--but might also be the very thing that will save your life and allow God's presence to become much more real in your life than it ever has been before. Maybe in the past, it was very appropriately a time for war between all of you. But there is one problem with that now--the war's over. Both of you have been gravely injured by this--why keep on fighting this war anymore, this war that has caused you both so much pain and heartache? It's time to lick our wounds and start the long, painful road to peace. The season of war is now about to thankfully come to an end--and it is now time for the season of peace for everyone concerned to begin.

It is interesting to know what time is it for something. We all look forward to the time when this or that will happen or dread the next time we do something wrong. Farmers consider carefully the proper time to plant or harvest their crops. Well, it seems that the tribe of Issachar provided this same service for David before he became King of Israel, as mentioned in the first part of First Chronicles 12:31: "...men of Issachar, who understood the times and knew what Israel should do..." All of this makes what King Solomon wrote in Ecclesiastes so much more poignant.

Before we park for a while for the rest of this lesson in the area of Ecclesiastes, maybe I feel the need to let you in on some times both in my past as well as in recent memory where this thing about "...a time for war and a time for peace" seems to resonate in my personal life and give you a bit more insight on the crucial need and pressing desire that we should have to earnestly seek reconciliation with those who have a cause against us--whether justified or unjustified.

Within the past few years, there have been rare situations in my own life in which the need for "...a time for war" was imminent. But just as important as knowing whether or not it is the time for war is the need to know when it is finally time to end the war and start the negotiations for peace. The tactics for each in terms of fighting each war were totally different--but I feel that the lessons of each conflict presented here will be universally applicable for all situations and will have some usefulness in everything that you might do and say.

The first of the conflicts involved a situation with a men's group I was at one time involved in. I had been meeting with them once a week on Monday nights for a while for about several months. But the last night that I was allowed to come there proved to be a real eye-opener for me and a lesson God taught me that I have never forgotten since.

At the time, I did not even conceive in my mind that it was going to be the last time I was going to meet with that group. And it didn't even dawn on me until later the implications of what was about to take place. Maybe I should have known that the tone was set the minute that one of the men as I was coming in to the church that we were meeting at made a remark about the son of the man who was the founder of one of the churches that I am personally a member of. The group consisted of at that time, besides myself, roughly half Baptists and the other half Pentecostals. One might truly say that I was pretty much considered the misfit of the whole group. By misfit, I mean that I was the ONLY one of that group who was NOT affiliated with either one of those two denominations--PLUS I was the ONLY one who DID NOT have a wife or kids AT ALL. This and other factors I discovered later on seemed to create some underlying tensions that others might have had against me that I wasn't even aware of.

But apparently the fact of the church I am a part of in which had previously had a reputation (both well-deserved as well as that of being unjustified) for being VERY legalistic in its application of certain Old Testament laws and holding to doctrines that were not even anywhere close to the rim of what the rest of orthodox Christianity believes. It had only been within the past few years beforehand that my own church had made DRASTIC changes to its belief system to conform to the standards of orthodox Christianity. But apparently the message to the folks had not necessarily gotten to them yet--and I was to realize too late that there were some misconceptions about me and my church that these men had that had not been truly and honestly addressed in an open forum.

What was interesting about this at first was that we actually had snacks and food there--something that was very rare for that meeting. It didn't seem strange to me at first--but now I think about what David said in Ps. 41:9 where he said, "Even my close friend, whom I trusted, he who shared my bread, has lifted up his heel against me." In the midst of eating Fritos, etc., we started the Bible study--and little did I know what was in store for me just up ahead.

At one point in the study, I remarked at something using the Keener commentary (in which has been one of the sources that I have also used for this study course) to comment on a certain passage of Scripture. One of the men then asked me, "Yeah, but what do YOU say about it?" I started explaining my position--but I didn't get a chance to finish my point. The storm of questions started--and the masks were taken off. Like it or not, the fight (if I could call it such in the spiritual realm) was on. And I very much in my spirit felt like a deer in the headlights of an oncoming semi-truck, frozen and unable to know how I could react to this sudden barrage of hostile comments against me.

All of this got eventually where the men even started doubting whether or not I was truly saved at all. The condemnation I felt then was so thick in that room that you could have cut it with a knife and sliced pieces off of it. And the pressure was so intense that it seemed like the ONLY way I could get out of that to prove that I was not who they said they were was to basically indulge them and pray the Sinner's Prayer to prove to them that I was not the problem (even though I did not seem to present it to them in that exact way at the time). But even then, it STILL did not satisfy them. As a result of this, you might as well say that I was summarily and unceremoniously kicked out of the group and not invited to come back.

When I got home, I literally cried to God and asked him for an explanation of what all of this was truly about. I literally for about two weeks hardly slept a wink, grieving and crying to God over this issue, and wondering if I was truly saved at all and if I truly had a personal relationship with Him. And somehow in my spirit, I eventually had enough discernment to know to make a decision that I would not speak to ANYONE involved with that group and even attempt to broach the subject about trying to get back into the group for fear that they might interpret it as an attempt from me to lobby them to get back in the group. Somehow, the thought came to my mind that I should do nothing in a way that would offend them or in which they might interpret as trying to get back into their good graces. I sensed that if my God wanted me to get back into the group that He would make a way and open the door to get back in without any effort on my part.

In this process, I also started the process of self-examination to first see if the problem was due to something that I had done personally and see if there be some wicked way in me that was deep down and needed to be exposed. I even asked the pastor of my church in the midst of this indirectly (without explaining to him the full situation, that is) as a way to verify what I in my heart truly knew about my standing and relationship with God. I asked him, "Whenever you counseled someone for baptism,in the past, I'm wondering about whether or not you did two things--one, did you preach salvation and the need to trust Christ as the sacrifice for their sins to anyone that you counseled? And two, did you talk to them about the need for repentance from sin and to turn away from those things which were wrong?" To both questions, he basically replied: "Absolutely. Definitely. Without a doubt. I did those things every time."

Afterwards, when I remembered the things that I had went through in the process of counseling for baptism and (even though encrusted with various additional requirements that I had to follow at the time) and looked back at the fact that the pastor who had the privilege of baptizing me and who helped me realize the saving grace and knowledge of our Lord, then and only then did I realize that the problem was not with me--but instead could be directly and partially attributed to a spiritual attack by the Adversary in making me doubt my salvation at all.

How was that? Well, just before that time, I with another man from a different nearby city had proposed that this same group possibly get involved with the creation of small groups within the nearby prison units in our area. When the group met to consider this proposal, the idea met with at best very tepid and lukewarm support by all of those involved. But nevertheless, they started the process of being involved with prison ministry--an effort that, from what I heard later on about this same group, went very strong for several years and has reaped many benefits ever since.

But unfortunately, it came at a high price for me whenever I was kicked oout of this group. Needless to say, I was still grieving over this loss of fellowship when one about several weeks later God spoke to my heart in a soft, reassuring voice in ways that were rare to me at that time. He said two things to me. The first one was: "Son, you don't worry about them. I'LL take care of them." But the second was the one that ministered to my heart more than anything else. He then said: "Son, when you did what you did six years ago, that was good enough for Me." What God was referring to was the process of conversion that I had made leading to baptism that enabled me to be a member of the church that I am still currently a member of.

To me, I for all practical purposes have ever since considered the date of my baptism the equivalent of my "spiritual birthday" of when I felt that I was truly born again and when I felt that my relationship with Him once and for all truly started. I took my vows so seriously to my God that I even thought of it as the day that I finally married God and the day that I put my invisible "wedding ring" on my finger that symbolized and reminded me of the deep, personal, and passionate commitment that I had made to my Savior for all eternity to come. [I even considered it so much more important that it took higher precedence to me than even my physical birthday and to where I even use that date more than anything else for such things as the PIN numbers that I use to access my bank account, etc. If a date holds THAT much significance that it is something that influences even the most routine of your financial transactions, you KNOW for sure that it has impact on you.] From then on, I did not actively seek to try to get back in that group or desire to try to impress them in any way. I instead started to make other plans personally for my Mon. nights that paid much higher dividends.

Maybe the war (if it really was one in the first place) that you have just went through was exactly like I just described. It came on you so unexpectedly that you had absolutely NO time to prepare for it and that, by the time you decided to face that situation head on, it was too late to do anything about it. You were, as I was, a deer in the headlights confused and scared about what to do next. You wanted so bad to fight back, but realized that if you did so, the problem you had would only get ten times worse if you stood up and tried to do something that would have allowed you to let off steam, but that no tangible results would have been gained from pursuing those tactics. If this is what describes you, then I know a little bit of just exactly what you feel.

But that's not all of the personal wars that I've had to fight in my own lifetime. I also remember one instance when I interviewed someone for the Internet forum that I used to write for. I was interviewing this man one time for a series of certain things happening within my state's criminal justice system. I originally didn't expect much other than a 1 to 2-hour interview, nothing too outstanding or unusual. But little did I know until it was too late and when everything was already said and done what, shall we say, "interesting" experiences this one interview would get me into later on.

I did the interview as best and as professional as I could in my normal manner as a journalist. But the interview I anticipated would take 1 to 2 hours to do wound up taking EIGHT hours to complete covering about 4 audiotapes of material. This man gave me enough materials for articles for SEVEN consecutive weeks--the most I had ever given any interview subject at a time. This seemed all good and well--that is, UNTIL...

Some situations happened to this man that eventually led to some major problems on my end. You see, this man was VERY close to his release from parole at the time-- and I originally slated that interview to be released AFTER he was officially released from parole. That was SUPPOSED to be the case--UNTIL he was arrested by the county sheriff's office. Then, in my process of preparing the articles for publication, some previously unknown information became available to me that literally shot holes through my interview subject's credibility. One source, for instance, told me that this man apparently had a penchant for threatening to sue people for libel, slander, and defamation of character if they even dared say ANYTHING that he did not like. Plus, one or two of the things that he mentioned during the course of the interview didn't exactly check out the way he said that they did. Also, one source even said that he had some possible knowledge that that man was also possibly involved with child pornography on the Internet. But what really got my brain turning is when one of the reporters who worked at the local newspaper that I knew very well told me of an incident that had happened several years earlier that alleged that this man may have technically been in violation of the terms of his parole because of his personal association with someone who had went on trial for some very serious offenses.

As is my duty as a journalist, I was obliged to reveal these details as a part of this interview. Nothing happened immediately after its publication--and I had basically laid the matter aside. THEN--about six months later, I happened to see this man at one of the places where I worked in town. He asked about the article--and I told him the URL where he could find it. If I had known then what I know now, I would NOT have given him that Web site address because not too long after that, he started sending me and the Internet forum I worked for some very threatening e-mails in regards to these articles and (as I was to find out later) had even posted some very disparaging e-mails about these things, causing a number of my fellow editors extreme anguish and upset. I tried to personally deal with him on this matter and even offered to take the time to resolve these issues with him personally face-to-face--but the threatening e-mails just continued until I could not realistically deal with him on my own anymore.

I remember so well the subject line of the e-mail I typed to my editor-in-chief in regards to the situation: "Re: A Time For War". There was no doubt where I feared all of this, despite my best efforts, would lead--in court. What was even more interesting about this is that the place I wrote for was based in Canada--thereby automatically also making it a matter of international law. What I hoped could have been resolved between myself and this man within the same city instead eventually involved a possible legal battle in TWO countries. Thankfully, the thing did not have to go to court thanks to a settlement that was reached by the lawyers on both sides. Unfortunately, the initial editorial commentary was eventually edited out by my editor-in-chief--but that to me was a small price to pay compared to having to deal with a major libel suit that would have not only cost me money that I did not have at the time personally, but even possibly a job.

The final results of it all were for me extremely bittersweet--the lawsuit was settled, but at a cost of what I had thought had been a good friendship. Life for me went back to some form of normalcy, but I was a LOT more careful and cautious later on with what I did with my future interview subjects. And the ultimate fate of the other party in this story? I eventually heard through various media in the area that he had pleaded guilty to several counts of the following: copyright infringement, unauthorized distribution of copyrighted materials, and (as I had originally suspected) activities related to child pornography on the Internet. This man who had once done over 10 years of time in my state's criminal justice system is now having to serve 17 1/2 years in federal prison. And the worst part of it is that he left behind a wife who has severe epileptic seizures with virtually no place to turn to for financial support and who I pray is not being forced to sleep on the streets of my city as we speak.

I also had another situation arise recently in which this "a time for war" thing was very apparent as well. For several years, I had been able to ride by an quasi-governmental organization what was a "fixed-route" bus here in the city where I live to get from one place to another locally. I and various other riders had seen, though, some things about what this certain service did that did not make much sense.at all. For one thing, the place that did their mechanical repairs did work that to even someone who is not an auto mechanic was extremely horrific work that even a for-profit taxicab service would not in their wildest dreams even think to use--thereby costing this organization who knows how many thousands of dollars. Also, certain members of the management and staff of this organization had, in our view, extremely mistreated the driver of the bus to what seemed a most intolerable point. And if that were not enough, the same staff had even done things to mistreat the clients that they served in the most inappropriate manner possible.

Finally, when they announced that the fixed route service was going to be completely eliminated, it proved to be the final straw that broke the camel's back for me. This incident then inspired me to send via e-mail a list of grievances and complaints against this organization to the immediate supervisor over the head of the local office of this organization. The next week, I had a meeting with the head of the local office for over an hour on these issues--in which we had a very candid and frank discussion of these issues--with even the driver of the "fixed-route" himself being present. The meeting ended with a positive result and what could have been a golden opportunity to get the issues resolved--or at least so I thought.

That was, until I found out from one of my contacts that support for my proposals to the local office had very much evaporated due to a lack of support from some of my fellow riders and what I might have personally considered--for lack of a better term--cowardice. It's always amazing to me just how many people gripe and complain about something constantly--but when the occasion comes that might give them an opportunity to actually do something about it, the same folks that you thought might have supported you were afraid to even be associated with it, much less get personally involved. As a result, I was forced to have to withdraw these grievances and find a way to bow out gracefully and save face while still urging the local office to still take these concerns seriously.

Yes, it seems that I have learned all too well the lessons that King Solomon said the following in Ecclesiastes 3:

"There is a time for everything, and a season for every
activity under heaven: a time to be born and a time to die,
an time to plant and a time to uproot, a time to kill and a
time to heal, a time to tear down and a time to build, a time

to weep and a time to laugh, a time to mourn and a time to dance, a time to scatter stones and a time to gether them, a time to embrace and a time to refrain, a time to search and a time to give up, a time to keep and a time to throw away, a time to tear and a time to mend, a time to be silent and a time to speak, a time to love and a time to hate, a time for war and a time for peace." [Ecclesiates 3:1-8, NIV]

All of this makes the Rav Shaul's comments to the Corinthians all the more painful clear and evident:
"So from now on we regard no one from a worldly point of view. Though we once regarded Christ in this way, we do so no longer. Therefore, if anyone is in Christ, he is a new creation; the old has gone, the new had come! All this is from God, who reconciled us to himself through Christ and gave us the ministry of reconciliation; that God was reconciling the world to himself in Christ, not counting men's sins against them. And he has committed to us the message pf reconciliation. We are therefore Christ's ambassadors, as though God were making his appeal through us. We implore you on Christ's behalf: Be reconciled to God. God made him who had no sin to be sin for us, so that in him we might become the righteousness of God." (2 Corinthians 5: 16-21, NIV]

Powerful words from a Jewish rabbi, huh? I think, though, that I could even dare stretch this further and add that our God is also simultaneously saying to us: "Also, while you're at it, why don't you be reconciled to each other, too?" Why would I dare say this? Because of something I know in my spirit seems to be a plain and simple fact with our God--it is HIS own very heart. IN FACT, He emphasized this point in MANY WAYS all throughout His holy Word that he even dared make it equal to our need to be reconciled to Him. In God's eyes, in otherwords--you cannot be truly reconciled to Him UNLESS AND UNTIL you first take the steps necessary to those you are not personally reconciled with (whether or not you are able to do it face-to-face with that person). And I don't say what I have just said only to be saying something...au contrare--I say this because maybe deep down in our spirit, it will shout definite, deep, and passionate agreement with that. And if even our spirit immediately recognizes that fact even if we are not otherwise cognizant of it, how much more that we should follow the Holy Spirit's lead in doing something that will put our own spirits at peace and that we know within us is the ONLY truly right thing that we should do?

Let me ask you something--what is usually the biggest major prerequisite that has to occur BEFORE a military conflict can be OFFICIALLY be considered to end?

Naturally, before the formal agreement is even signed by the major dignitaries present with a lot of hoopla surrounding it, hours, days, weeks, months, even years of intense negotiation and hard work has to go in by both sides before such a treaty or agreement can even be created, much less signed and agreed to by both parties. Extra time and care has to be taken that both sides are aware of what the possible ramifications and effects of such an agreement are BEFORE both parties sign on the dotted line. If one party balks at a certain provision, the WHOLE ENTIRE process stops unless and until mutually acceptable terms to both parties can be agreed to without reservation.

To both the victim and offender--you have gone through this course so far trying to find out what the other side has went through and the things that they think about in their minds. You have went through the pain of grieving for your losses and have now made your adjustments to move on with what is left of your life. But now I feel that there is at least one thing more that BOTH of you must do--or all of the time, energy, etc. I have personally spent on the creation of this course has been in vain.

If you now cannot take the leap of faith required of you to bury the hatchet you now have with the other side--if you cannot personally be willing to forgive and to work to leave the past behind you that the two of you have shared and instead establish a new relationship built on trust, faith, confidence, and, most of all, the very love that our Savior/Meshiach has given us--then this war will continue to haunt you until you either finally decide to come to grips with it OR until you are in the grave. And the worst part of it all is the miserable and unhappy life that you will personally live between those times.

It's time for closure now. No, I cannot even dare try to turn back the hands of time in a way in which we could erase the incident and pretend that it never existed in the first place. But if there is one way above all else that I could be of service to the very God that I serve, it is this--to help bring a sense of closure to both of you and to help in some way turn what our Adversary meant for harm into something that our God can turn from good and that would honor and exalt His holy name. That is the very act of turning people who once were enemies of each other into friends, brothers, and sisters in Him.

This, though, will be the VERY thing that the Adversary DOES NOT want to see happen--and he will do everything possible to hinder and/or stop it completely. But you must nevertheless resist the urge and instead listen to God's own heart in the matter: "We implore you on Christ's behalf: Be reconciled to God." And also--that you be reconciled to each other. The time for war is over and long past--and it is high time for the time for peace to begin. It's now THE appointed time to sign a covenant of peace that BOTH parties can agree to, bury the hatchet, resolve the differences between them, and move on with our lives in the way that our God desires for us to do. If we will sign a treaty of peace with each other AND agree to abide by it, then we will not only be listening to our own both deep and inward selfish yearnings--but we will be also be simultaneously listening to God's own heart and voice in the process. And from there, our song and our joy will finally take wing. "'Come now, let us reason together,' says the LORD. 'Though your sins are like scarlet, they shall be as white as snow; though they are read as crimson, they shall be like wool. If you are willing and obedient, you will eat the best from the land; but if you resist and rebel, you will be devoured by the sword.' For the mouth of the LORD has spoken." [Isa. 1:18-20, NIV] Let's now sign the following peace treaty together and get this thing behind us.

DISCUSSION AND HOMEWORK: The assignment is simple--look over the terms of the peace treaty that follows and think and meditate upon them. And if you possibly can, get with the other party in your dispute (no matter what it is all about) and have a signing ceremony IN FRONT OF WITNESSES that will show to the world that you are serious about what you are about to do here:

FORMAL AGREEMENT OF RECONCILIATION AND RESTORATION

LET IT HEREBY BE KNOWN to all that the following parties described below have of their own free will and volition without undue pressure from any outside forces AND in love and obedience to the Lord God Almighty (to be hereby referred to as the Father), the Lord Jesus Christ/Yeshua Ha'Meshiach (to be hereby referred to as the Son), and the Comforter/Ruach Ha'Kodesh/Holy Spirit [to be hereby referred to as the Spirit] and in their desire to fall in line with the dictates and precepts of holy Scripture--have formally decided to sign this FORMAL AGREEMENT OF RECONCILIATION AND RESTORATION (to be hereby known as Agreement) and publicly announce to the world that all hostilities still remaining between the parties will now and forever cease and that the parties entering into this Agreement now formally resolve to start the long, painful process of the appropriate settlement of all remaining disputes and conflicts between the parties.

This agreement and covenant is made between _____ (to be hereby known as Victim) and _____ (to be hereby known as

Offender) and is also automatically considered understood that upon the signing of this Agreement that the above mentioned Father, Son, and Spirit will also be considered parties to this Agreement. The provisions of such an Agreement include (but are not limited) to:

SECTION I: That Victim, Offender, and all other parties directly involved in the signing of such an Agreement understand that the provisions of such an Agreement SHALL NOT supercede the requirements and dictates of any local, state, or federal laws and will not have any legal effect on such existing laws--and that thereby as such, all parties are still considered legally bound to abide with such decisions that any such appropriate governmental entity shall make and that this Agreement shall, by necessity, be constrained, defined, and confined by such decisions by those governmental entities directly involved;

SECTION II: That the Agreement that has been reached here is only meant to serve as an aid within the healing process of reconciliation between Victim and Offender and that, as a result, that all parties involved shall appropriately maintain REASONABLE expectations of any possible effects from this Agreement and WILL NOT therefore place any undue and unnecessary obligations on such an Agreement and will not hold any intermediaries and/or officials directly or indirectly responsible for any breach or failure to uphold any such provisions of this Agreement;

SECTION III: That all parties involved will assume FULL responsibility for their personal part in the upholding of the provisions of this Agreement and that undue aspersions, gossip, inappropriate comments, blame, etc. SHALL NOT be unnecessarily made towards any party involved in the creation of this Agreement should any party in any way knowingly or unknowingly breach or fail to uphold any provision of this Agreement;

SECTION IV: EXPECTATIONS OF PARTIES INVOLVED BY THE FATHER, SON, AND SPIRIT

Both Victim and Offender recognize and realize that the Father, Son, and Spirit have certain expectations and obligations placed upon the parties entering into this Agreement in order for this Agreement to be properly considered in their eyes a valid and binding Agreement for reconciliation and restoration. Such provisions include (but are not limited to):

(a.) Recognition for the need for reconciliation and restoration of fellowship between Victim and Offender (Matt. 5:24);

(b.) Recognition of the vital role that the Son played through His death on the cross as an acceptable atonement and reconciliation for the sins of BOTH parties against the Father (Lev. 8:15 AND ALL of chap. 16: ; 2 Chron. 29: ; Ezek. 45:15; Rom. 5:10; 2 Cor. 5:18-20; Col. 1:21; Heb. 2:17);

(c.) Recognition that BOTH parties have in various ways knowingly or unknowingly trespassed against one another in various ways and that therefore the Father, Son, and Spirit take these offenses VERY seriously and are EXTREMELY grieved over the trespasses of either or both parties; [(Ex.) Lev. chapters 18-20]

(d.) Recognition by both parties that the continuance of such trespasses and the subsequent conflict that has resulted from them may also put in serious danger and jeopardy each party's individual relationship with the Father, Son, and Spirit [Matt. 5:21-26];

(e.) A FORMAL recognition and declaration by BOTH parties that each has EQUALLY sinned and come short of the glory of the Father, Son, and Spirit and that each party entering into this Agreement is now sorry for the sins that they have committed against the Father, Son, and Spirit and against others and is now TRULY repentant for the sins they have committed against the Father, Son, and Spirit and is now seeking forgiveness from the Father, Son, and Spirit for such actions committed against them and hereby wishes and resolves to appropriately turn away from such violations in the future as best as they are able and attempt to the best of his/her ability to work towards reconciling and making appropriate restitution towards others that he/she has offended as he/she has appropriate opportunity to do so AND in the event that he/she may possibly in the future make such violations of ANY kind against the Father, Son, and Spirit that he/she will then immediately again humbly repent and seek the forgiveness and mercy so abundantly available through the Father as a result of the sacrifice of His only Son;

(f.) That BOTH parties recognize that in the eyes of the Father, Son, and Spirit that no party should henceforth be considered superior or inferior to each other as far as how the Father, Son, and Spirit may possibly perceive the other party's personal relationship to the Father, Son, and Spirit in comparison to their own and that each party is looked upon in the SAME EXACT way that the Father, Son, and Spirit looks upon the rest of humanity currently residing on this planet;

SECTION V: DECLARATIONS OF THE OFFENDER
The Offender now declares through his/her signing of this Agreement the following:

(a.) That Offender now fully recognizes that an offense has been committed against the Victim and that Offender is fully responsible for such an offense against the Victim;

(b.) That Offender now fully recognizes the FULL and TOTAL impact that the offense that Offender was responsible in committing against Victim and that Victim has suffered irreparable damage, harm, loss of various kinds, emotional trauma, injury, etc. as a result of the offense and is now more understanding of the effects of such an offense against the Victim;

(c.) That Offender hereby FORMALLY acknowledges the FULL responsibility for the offense that Offender committed against Victim and FORMALLY seeks from the Victim FORMAL forgiveness, mercy, and compassion for what Offender has done to the Victim and also the opportunity to FORMALLY seek a restitution and reconciliation with them in regards to this matter and an opportunity for involvement (if possible) for a new and better relationship of some kind WITH appropriate boundaries that will be now agreed to by both parties (as will be referred to later in this Agreement) and that will henceforth be conducted in a manner that lines up in accordance to the will of the Father, Son, and Spirit and that does not violate IN ANY WAY the dictates of Holy Scripture;

(d.) That the Offender hereby pledges to Victim that all appropriate efforts on his/her behalf (as long as it is done in an appropriate manner and does not otherwise violate the dictates of Holy Scripture and/or existing local, state, or federal laws and/or prevailing court orders against either party) to make appropriate restitution of some kind to Victim in a manner that BOTH adheres to existing laws by all governmental entities directly or indirectly involved and that is satisfactory and agreeable to the Victim;

(e.) That the Offender wishes to declare and make known to the Victim that he/she will plan to appropriately respect the wishes, desires, and privacy of Victim in the future and will not expect, desire, or demand that Victim do anything for the Offender that Victim finds uncomfortable, offensive, or disconcerting to himself/herself and that Offender from here on out shall work to appropriately act towards the Victim in a civilized, respectful, and dignified manner that will have as its utmost priority a true concern for the well-being and welfare of Victim in mind:

SECTION VI: DECLARATIONS OF THE VICTIM

The Victim now declares through his/her signing of this Agreement the following:

(a.) That Victim is now more fully cognizant of the specific background and history of Offender and what may have led Offender to commit such violations against the Victim;

(b.) That Victim also recognizes that as a result of the offense that he/she may have possibly harbored certain bitterness, hatred, and resentment against Offender since the time of the offense and acknowledges responsibility for harboring such things against the Offender and therefore humbly states his/her sorrow for harboring such things in his/her heart towards the Offender and also asks the Offender for his/her forgiveness and mercy in regards to these things;

(c.) That Victim appropriately recognizes that each of these emotions mentioned in (b.) are valid ones and not ones to be ashamed of in itself to express or communicate--but that such things should also be dealt with if ANY healing is to take place at all in regards to any future relations with the Offender;

(d.) That Victim recognizes that he/she is not obliged or obligated to do ANYTHING for or on behalf of the Offender in ANY WAY that might make the Victim uncomfortable, disconcerted, inappropriate, or suspicious and that Victim is NOT to be blamed in ANY way, shape, or form for the offenses and actions committed by the Offender and that Victim IS NOT RESPONSIBLE in ANY WAY for what Offender did towards the Victim and absolves himself/herself from any blame in regards to the offense committed by the Offender;

(e.) That Victim FULLY and UNCONDITIONALLY recognizes the FULL validity of Offender's plea and request for forgiveness for the offense committed against Victim (as previously described in Section V) and is fully discerning of Offender's desire for reconciliation and restoration of fellowship and relationship in spite of the offense that Offender has committed against Victim;

(f.) That Victim, from his/her own free will and volition AND WITHOUT undue pressure from any outside forces, hereby declares through the signing of this Agreement his/her forgiveness and pardon of any inappropriate actions and offenses of the Offender committed against Victim and his/her willingness to work with the Offender towards appropriate requirements for restitution on the part of the Offender towards the Victim, appropriate boundaries for any future relationship that Offender and Victim might have with each other, and the general reconciliation and restoration of fellowship and relationship that Victim and Offender may have with each other in the future;

(g.) That Victim will also resolve to CLEARLY and EXPLICITLY communicate to the Offender ANY stipulations, requirements, and expectations that the Victim may have of the Offender so that Offender may subsequently be more fully able to work towards appropriate restitution, reconciliation, and restoration of his/her relationship towards the Victim in the future;

SECTION VII: MAJOR OBLIGATIONS AND STIPULATIONS OF THIS AGREEMENT

As a part of this Agreement, Victim and Offender hereby FORMALLY resolve to perform the following stipulations and obligations:

(a.) That Offender and Victim will negotiate and agree to mutually acceptable boundaries and requirements for a future relationship with each other in a manner that is both acceptable to the wishes of the Father, Son, and Spirit and that also adheres and complies to the requirements of all applicable local, state, and federal laws;

(b.) That Offender and Victim henceforth agree to respect the needs, desires, wishes, and privacy of the other party involved in this Agreement and work towards treating the other party in a respectful, civilized, dignified, and loving manner;

(c.) That Offender and Victim will henceforth work to CLEARLY and EXPLICITLY communicate their expectations, etc. of the other party and NOT place undue burdens, obligations, etc. upon the other party outside those EXPLICITLY spelled out in

this Agreement;

(d.) That Offender and Victim understand that should one party violate any term of this Agreement in a manner that is not acceptable to the other party, that the party that is to be found in breach of or in failure to uphold the terms of this Agreement will AUTOMATICALLY understand that the party that was offended will maintain the right to seek whatever means of recourse that might be available to him/her--even possibly civil or criminal prosecution by appropriate governmental authorities if the offended party may deem necessary;

(e.) That Offender and Victim hereby agree to as much as possible NOT to make UNREASONABLE demands and expectations on the other party that are in ANY way, shape, or form that are not either otherwise EXPLICITLY spelled out in this Agreement and that might unduly, unreasonably, and inappropriately make the other party feel uncomfortable and demeaned as a person if the demand DOES NOT directly and otherwise impact the adherence to the specific terms of this Agreement;

(f.) That, to help further facilitate the process of healing of both parties, Offender and Victim after the signing of this Agreement will have NO further direct or indirect contact with each other OTHER than through mutually and specifically authorized third-parties AND in adherence to the wishes of such third-party agents in specifically constructed environments and conditions that might be created by such third-parties for a period of NO LESS than six months after the signing of this Agreement and lasting NO LONGER than a year so that the gradual establishment and adjustment to such mutually agreed-upon boundaries by both parties can properly take place and so that appropriate counseling of both parties by such designated third-party agents to help in the process of reconciliation and restoration can take place to further ease and expedite this period of transition and readjustment;

(g.) That should both parties eventually desire a sort of deeper APPROPRIATE friendship after the transition period that Offender and Victim would have suitable boundaries in place as far as how the future of such a relationship should go;

(h.) That BOTH parties agree NOT, during the course of this transition period, to enter into ANY kind of INAPPROPRIATE romantic, marital, and/or sexual relationship with each other as well as ANY possible form of relationship [(Ex.) Business transactions, financial obligations, legal obligations, etc.] that may otherwise hinder the original purpose and intent of this Agreement and that is otherwise in violation of all local, state, and federal laws and does not otherwise adhere to the prohibitions of Holy Scripture and the wishes of the Father, Son, and Spirit, and that might otherwise cause unnecessary complications and conflict to the process of reconciliation and restoration of the relationship between Offender and Victim;

SECTION VII: OTHER MISCELLANEOUS CONDITIONS, STIPULATIONS, AND REQUIREMENTS BETWEEN THE PARTIES

The Offender and Victim have also agreed to abide by the following conditions, stipulations, and requirements that they have negotiated and agreed to with each other as stated here:

SECTION VIII: That this Agreement between the parties shall be considered in effect and in force IMMEDIATELY after the signing of this Agreement by the affected parties AND appropriately witnessed by other third-party agents that are directly involved in the development and negotiations of this Agreement and the terms of this Agreement be considered IMMEDIATELY binding upon all parties involved;

SECTION IX: That should a dispute arise at any time over the validity, enforcement, etc. in regards to any provision of this Agreement that any third-party agents involved in the negotiation process be also charged with the duty of assisting in the enforcement of such provisions during the transition period as mentioned above; and then if such disputes arise after the end of the transition period that the affected parties will be solely responsible to come up with an adequately satisfactory decision between the parties OR to seek other means of recourse in solving such disputes;

SECTION X: That should there need to be an amendment in the terms of this Agreement, the affected parties would then work to negotiate with each other to arrive at the inclusion of such an amendment within the terms of this Agreement;

Let it be hereby known that the affected parties have FULLY read, understood, and consented to the terms of this Agreement out of their own free will and volition and that this Agreement is thereby ratified and declared in effect between the parties on this date, _____, by the declaration of each party in writing through their signatures:

_____ Victim

_____ Offender

We each officially declare on this date of _____ that we have witnessed the signing and execution of the above Agreement and can attest to the validity of this Agreement entered into by the affected parties. This we each declare with our own hands in writing through our signatures:

_____ Witness 1

_____ Witness 2

_____ Witness 3

UNIT IV, LESSON 2--The Road From Here: It's a HARD Row To Hoe

Now at this place in time, the journey through your own personal Siberia is now beginning to come to a close. The road that you've traveled so far in the process has not been an easy one by any means. BUT GUESS WHAT??? God now wants me to give you this word of encouragement as our studies on these topics winds toward a close: YOU'VE MADE IT!! The very fact that our God--YOUR God--has graciously and gently led you out of the barren land you have traveled should be enough of a witness and testimony of God's love, concern, and mercy to you and also evidence to others that nothing is too hard for our God.

But now the hardest part of all this lies just ahead. The gates of the Siberian prison you've been incarcerated in for a while are finally swinging open wide for you. Your exile is finally over--and at last, you're free to go. But now a new question arises-- where does the road go from here? And what happens now?

One thing will be for sure--it'll definitely take some time to get used to being free again. It will not be a rose garden by any means--in fact, the future will seem like a much harder row for you to hoe than even the horrific journey that you've just been recently forced to go through. And absolutely NOTHING that I could ever say can take the hurt and pain of the past away--for that is something that only your merciful God can do for you (if you will only allow Him to do so in HIS due time and season).

But maybe something that I can say here will at least provide you with a little bit of assurance and confidence as you travel on away from the prison gates and go homeward bound. Contrary to what you might believe, there is even a reason for the chaos and torture you've went through. God DOES have some use even for this stuff that still does not make sense to you. NO--my God DID NOT give you this to "teach you a lesson". He is NOT to blame for the devastation that only comes from the Adversary. But this also doesn't mean that the Father cannot incorporate and weave this as a part of the patchwork quilt of your life. And it certainly doesn't mean that the ugliness, shame, and ashes that you have been handed cannot be turned into a delicately and intricately handwoven piece of art that is a dazzling and mind-blowing work of immense beauty.

But our God doesn't stop here. IN fact, He sure doesn't want you to stop and park where you're at right now. As one song might put it, "He didn't bring you this far just to leave you." You've come this far by faith--but your journey of healing and restoration should never stop here. The road still goes on--and you have a new life to live now. Siberia's behind you now--it's time to leave the past behind for good and go on to the good things our God has in store for you in the road just up ahead. Your Jordan is waiting for you to cross. The land you're entering into now is a good land full of promise. It's time now to go in and conquer it.

After all the times in recent studies that we've used our DISCUSSION QUE$TIONS to deal with negative things, I want to use them now as a way to see for yourself a major message of encouragement and strength to prepare and bolster you for the road ahead. Let's use this session, in a sense, as a final pep rally that God wants to give you as a good and proper sendoff for the road from here that lies ahead:

[DISCUSSION QUESTIONS:]

(1.) Let's take a quick look at Joshua chapters 1-6. Read and skim through them for a few minutes, then answer the following questions:

(a.) (***) (1:6-9) What word did the Lord give Joshua before they entered the Promised Land?

_____

(b.) (1:10-18) What orders did Joshua give the people of Israel before crossing the Jordan?

_____

(c.) (Chapter 2) What seems to be the predominant theme of this chapter? What do you see to be the things that are most important about this chapter?

_____

(d.) (Chapters 3 & 4) Was there a miracle that God performed for the Israelites here? If so, what was it?

_____

[(NOTE:) The Promise Keepers Bible gives an interesting insight about what happened here in Chapter 4:

"...As Israel crossed the Jordan in fulfillment of God's promise of a new homeland, God commanded that his people remember His faithfulness. He told them to build a memorial to remind them of this day, and gave three reasons why. First, so that the people's children would learn from the things God did in their lives (vv.6-21). Second, so that other people who didn't know God would see his power at work in the life of Israel (v. 24). Third, as a personal and abiding reminder to fear God above all (v. 24).

"...As you reflect on the way God's Sovereign Hand has led you through your life, don't miss the marker events. Use them as testimonies to God's power and grace at work in you. Allow them to stand as reminders to you and your children, and as solid examples of God's power to those who do not know Him yet." (p. 227)]

(e.) (5:1-9) What is significant about Gilgal here? And how might it relate to your current situation?

_____

(f.) (5:13-6:20) What was the battle strategy that Joshua and the Israelites were told to use against Jericho? What were they advised to do?

_____

(g.) (6:19-27) What was the final result of the battle? What was the end of the story all about?

_____

(h.) (6:22 & 23) What about Rahab and her family? What happened to them?

_____

(i.) But the book of Joshua isn't the only place where Rahab is mentioned. What do the following Scriptures say about her?

Ps. 80:10 AND 87:4
Heb. 11:31
Isaiah 51:9
James 2:25
Matt. 1:5

[Note clearly in particular at the reference in Matthew 1: What do you notice most about Rahab there? [Hint: This involves the very genealogy of Christ Himself.]]

(II.) The book of Job seems to have a few things to say about suffering and why it seems to come into our lives. Let's dive in a little bit and learn a few lessons from this good man.

(a.) (Chapters 1 & 2) What happened to Job? What tests was he required to encounter?

_____

(b.) (1:6-12 AND 2:1-6) Who was the REAL instigator of all this? What did the Lord do in response? And why do you think God might take such an action?

_____

[NOTE: The PK Bible suggests five reasons how God even uses suffering to help accomplish His will and purposes in our lives:

(1.) **To develop character**--James 1 teaches that "...the testing of your faith develops perseverance." IF we remain true to God through the suffering process we will be "...mature and complete, not lacking anything" (James 1:1-4).
(2.) **To demonstrate the nature of our character**--Job was God's demonstration to Satan that there was a man who truly loved him and was truly righteous (Job 1:1-6). No matter what cruelty Satan devised, THIS man, God said, would endure in his righteousness.
(3.) **To allow God to demonstrate the strength he makes available to us** (2 Corinthians 12:7-10)--Paul was greatly blessed by God; he was a truly good man. He wrote that his suffering was God's way of keeping him dependent on God. The "...thorn in his flesh" helped him understand that God was sufficient for all his needs.
(4.) **To test us**--Genesis 22...describes the process by which God perfected Abraham's faith. Both the story in Genesis and God's explanation of it in James 2:20-24 tell us that God was showing Abraham what Abraham was made of.
(5.) **To discipline and correct us**--All people, even the most Godly among us, sin. Proverbs 3:11-12 and Hebrews 12:4-11 tell us that God uses suffering to guide us back to His way when we stray from it. Both passages show God as a loving Father who wants to correct behavior that will destroy us if we persist in it. Throughout Scripture, God deals with sin; not to vindictively punish us, but to lovingly correct us.

"...God's people must use their minds and attempt to understand all He has revealed. But God knows that the finite sometimes slams into the infinite; we cannot grasp all he is doing. At that point, God trusts our faith to keep us coming back to Him.

In the final analysis the question of why good people suffer has reasonable explanations, but, for many, no sufficient answer. Where the intellect boggles, faith in God's sovereign love must step in. The story of Job with all his pain, is not only a story of one man's faith in God's love, it is an exercise of man's faith in God's love. It will be so for you if you read it as it was written." (p. 549)

(c.) (2:7-10) What did Job's wife encourage him to do? And how did Job respond to it?

_____

(d.) (2:11 through the end of Chapter 37) Job's three friends and even another younger man, Elihu, have a pretty long discussion and discourse with Job on what's happened to Job. In skimming through these passages real quickly, some questions come to mind:

(1.) What did Job's friends and Elihu seem to constantly accuse Job of? Do they seem to infer that Job had done something wrong to cause these calamities to happen?

_____

(2.) What was Job's general response to it all?

_____

(3.) Did the comments of the three friends ease Job's pain or make it worse? And why do you say this?

_____

(4.) How might all of this relate to your own current situation? How can what other people say to you about your situation affect you? What should you do in response? What if the person who makes the comment about you makes it in ignorance? What should you do then? How can you truly determine whether a certain piece of advice that someone else may give might be helpful or not? And how can you tell the difference between what might be beneficial to you and what is not?

_____

(e.) What seems to typify Job's central reaction in the trials he faces? (13:15-19; 19:25-27)

_____

(f.) (Chapter 36:) THEN God enters into the picture and finally speaks to Job Himself. What does He say to him?

_____

(g.) (40:3-5 and 42:1-6) How does Job respond to God's intense round of questioning?

_____

(h.) (42:7 to the end) And what was, as Paul Harvey likes to say, "...the rest of the story" for Job?

_____

(i.) After looking over the panorama of the book of Job, what would YOU say about why suffering of any kind comes into our life and what God's role in this process might truly be?

_____

(III.) Now let's look toward the future. What might God advise you through His Word as to what you should know and what you should do from here?

(a.) What might God say through Jeremiah about what He has in mind for your life? (Jeremiah 29:10-14)

_____

(b.) Again, let's remember...What did the Lord command Joshua to be? (Joshua 1:6-9)

_____

(ALSO: In the above verses, several forms of this command appear AT LEAST 3 times within a span of four verses. What is the command that the Lord seem to want to get across to YOU most of all in this passage?)

(c.) Our Savior also commands us to do something as well. What does He Himself ask us to do? (Matt. 11:28-30)

_____

(d.) The writer of Proverbs also adds another good idea of wisdom here. What does He advise? And what does he mean by this? (Proverbs 3:5 & 6)

_____

(3.) The Rav Shaul/Apostle Paul went through many hardships in his life. Yet, God used him as an example for us to follow in how we should view hardship and suffering--whether it is in the past, present, or future. Let's ask him ourselves what he would recommend how we should view these things:

(1.) Check through these passages from Acts and comment briefly on them:

14:1-7 _____

16:15-40 _____

17:1-8 _____

21:17 through 28:16 _____

(2.) What seemed to be Paul's overall attitude about all the things he faced and went through? (Check 2 Cor. 4:7 & 8; Rom. 8:18-20; 2 Tim. 1:3 through 2:13; and 2 Cor. 1:3-11!)

_____

(3.) But Paul wasn't the only one in the New Testament who spoke about suffering--James did, too. What does James add to this discussion? (James 1:2-18)

_____

(4.) And Peter wants to chime in here, too. What rich harmony does Peter add to this subject of our relationship to suffering and how it should impact our view of God? (1 Pet. 4:12-19)

_____

(5.) But no matter where you go or what you do, as your Siberian prison disappears, fades out of sight in your rear view mirror, and becomes a distant memory of your past, the Savior Himself wishes to remind you of the last prayer HE prayed for Himself, His disciples, and even for you in John chapters 15 through 17. (Read over these real quick before we conclude.)

I think, though, above all else that the Savior is even now saying this over you: "I have told you these things, so that in Me you may have peace. In this world you will have trouble. But take heart! I have overcome the world." (John 16:33)

Steven Curtis Chapman wrote this chorus in the song "Remember Your Chains" off his "Heaven In The Real World" album: "Remember your chains/Remember the prison that once held you/Before the love of God brought you through/Remember the place you were without grace/When you see where you are now/Remember your chains/And remember your chains are gone."

As you say goodbye for good to Siberia, I'll only ask one thing of you as you head back towards home, your friends, and your family. Don't forget the lessons that you learned here in Siberia--but please don't ever come back here to stay here, neither. You have a much better place to look forward to anyway--and why would you want to go back to a place that offers nothing for you now? Go on to the hope that lies before you--and I'll see you and try to meet with you as soon as I get there myself. Enjoy the ride and have a safe trip. And tell the folks back home hi for me when you finally see them again.

[HOMEWORK:] It's time to plan your trip home and start thinking about the future now. Take some time to write our your answers to the following questions:

(1.) Where do you plan to go from here? What's the next goal on the agenda that you wish to accomplish?

(2.) How do you REALISTICALLY plan to get there? What is your step-by-step plan to get from Point A to B and then B to C...etc.?

(3.) BUT MOST IMPORTANTLY: How does GOD fit into your plans? What if the plans you've made don't exactly fit in with what HE truly wants for you? If those plans may not conform to His, then could you possibly consider changing YOUR plans to suit His? (Isa. 55:8 & 9)

[PRAYER:] Creator Father, Lord God Almighty, and Lord Jesus/Y'shua: I thank you today for all that You have done for me during this journey through my spiritual Siberia. Help me not to forget the many valuable lessons that I learned while I was here. But at the same time, please keep me from coming back here ever again to this place and instead help me move forward in You and to lead me on to better places than I have never even dared to dream of. And lead me on homeward bound to the richness of Your grace and mercy that lies ahead for me. I thank You, praise You, and lift Your name on high as MY Redeemer who forever lives and loves me. And I truly love You with all my heart for all of the things you have done for me in Siberia and that you will continue to do as I continue on the road from here. I say this in the name of your Son, Y'shua Ha'Meshiach/the Lord Jesus Christ--AMEN!!

UNIT IV, LESSON 3: A Message From Siberia--Whom The Son Sets Free Is Free Indeed

Most ministries always wonder why God brings people through the experiences they have faced. They debate over things like "mission statements", "vision-casting", and high-falluting terms like this. But I'm not one who normally likes to talk about those type of things. WHY? Because I personally see in part a reason more than ever why my God has allowed me to go through some unexplainable and unimaginable circumstances. Why was I raised a only child of a single mother who herself went through divorce? Why in tarnations would some dreams of mine have been broken and shattered in pieces at certain times in my life while at other times some of the most miraculous provisions of restoration in the face of uncertain times have been given to me without a fight? To these questions, it's VERY hard to give a reasonable explanation.

Why am I still here while others have fallen? I honestly don't know. But maybe now in hindsight, I see a deeper reason for why I do what I do here. To some, I will be brutally honest and say that I have not walked the exact road you have been on and will never fully understand what you are going through personally right now. You would be justified in calling me a liar if I said otherwise.

But maybe a big reason that I am here can be capsulized in the final time that we have together. If there has been no other message that you have received in the time that you shave studied what is at best a very BRIEF course that can only reasonably give you a pitiful foundational knowledge of the subjects of the effects of domestic violence and sexual assault on all of us and God's EXTREMELY DESPERATE desire for ALL parties to be reconciled--I pray that this message which follows (and that, by the way, is what I feel THE capstone message and most pressing thing that I must say to you right now) will definitely minister and be of some use to you.

How can I describe to you what these two (for lack of a better term) MONSTERS do to the fabric of a society? The only thing that in my opinion could be worse is the horrors that the Jewish people went through during the Holocaust and World War II. I was not even conceived or in at existence at this time, but I do have a indirect personal connection to WWII through my grandfather who served in a tank battalion in the Army in southern France and Germany during that war.

But I only have to think of hearing about the film "Schindler's List" Steven Speilberg made about the German businessman Oskar Schindler who during the war was probably at best a very reluctant person that was not at first very willing to be involved in anything outside of his own immediate business interests--and then later finding that despite the lives that he may have had a small hand in saving and that the people that he did save gave him a major gift of sacrifice in grateful appreciation--the ultimate outcome for him was the specter of bankruptcy that befell his business and what seems to be regretful cries of "I could have done more...I could have done more."

In this effort, I feel that I am in a similar position. The ROOT problems of domestic violence and sexual assault only give us what amounts to be a silent holocaust--and we in the Christian community have been silent about these topics for far too long (or--to our very shame--even worse, contributing further to the problem). But nevertheless I struggle to find the best way to explain this. Maybe one last extended personal story--my final message, if you will, from Siberia--may also wrap up our brief exploration of what we have discussed in these previous lessons.

You're probably asking me, "What in the heck are you talking about when you talk about Siberia?" If you take a brief look back in your history books at the history of Communist Russia, one of the Russian regions closest to the Arctic and to the U.S. state of Alaska named Siberia was used by that country's government as a massive prison camp to send those people into exile that the government considered to be "subversives", dangerous criminals, and/or those who disagreed in ANY way with the government's political views.

Maybe another place that might be even more torturous to the spirit is the prison of Alcatraz where the worst criminals of our nation were once kept. The worst part for those prisoners, according to some sources, was the very close distance from that island prison to the Golden Gate Bridge and San Francisco Bay. Whenever a prisoner could look out of the outside window and hear the sounds of partygoers and others across the Bay, it only increased their isolation because it was like they were so close to society, but yet so far away from it.

I definitely have never lived in Russia or have literally stayed in Alcatraz--but in my life so far to this date, I feel that I have went through the spiritual effects of both. Were it not for the grace of my God and His provision, I honestly doubt how long my hope and faith in Him as well as my physical life could have been sustained in any way, shape, or form.

Somehow, I sense in my spirit that those of you that are going through what seems to be a God-ordained process of recovery that this would describe you to a T, too. You do not care what others are saying around you--you are going through a spiritual

Vietnam followed immediately by a spiritual exile in Siberia on top of it. You are right now going through things that even some combat-hardened Vietnam and other war veterans could not even last two seconds in--and you are now going through utter despair and hopelessness and have way beyond gone past giving up hope that things will ever change for the better.

But the message I want to leave in this final section ABOVE ALL ELSE to you is the very fact that whenever everything has been tried and failed miserably, the God that I serve delights in and loves to make a way where there is no way. Even in the holocausts of our lives, even in Vietnam, and yes--even in the Siberian tundra--when dreams have been shattered and broken, promises not kept, and people have turned their back on you--the God that you think is now absent from all that you do is actually the same God who desires to move heaven and earth for you and who gave all that He could give to save your soul from everlasting judgment through His very Son who died on the cross for you. That God is VERY anxious to lead you out of your Siberian prison and into His marvelous, glorious light--if you will only allow Him to.

What is this spiritual Siberia like? It is, to say the least, a very unpleasant place to be. But please allow me anyway to take you on a brief walking tour in your mind of a place I once lived in and give you a few lessons from this place that I learned that might serve as parallels for what you are going through. (A preliminary hint to understanding all of this--think of it a lot like the process someone may have to go through in recovering from the loss of a spouse, close family member, or significant friend in their life.)

TOUR STOP #1--THE VALLEY OF SHOCK AND SURPRIZE

Our tour of spiritual Siberia starts just before I left Albuquerque. I have referred to my experiences there in other parts of this book--but I unfortunately didn't get to finish my story until now. I pick up the story from the time I was in the hospital recouperating from cataract surgery on my right eye.

The only ones from my church that even came to visit me in the hospital or that even knew of my situation were the same associate pastor and Spokeman's Club friend that were literally guiding my hand there during the remaining time I was in Albuquerque. I had asked my pastor to call my family to let them know that I was having the surgery--and he did so. My mother and grandparents came all the way to Albuquerque to see me in the hospital (which now I am very thankful that they did in spite of my horrific attitude towards them at the time). They urged me to come back home--but I was very unwilling to at that time because my personal desire was to try to fight the situation as best as I could. Sad to say, I regretfully treated them in a disrespectful manner. They gave me what I now realize was probably an easier way out of that situation--but I was so stubborn and set in my ways that I absolutely refused to take that road. Little did I know then that the very road that I did not want to go (even if I was dragged kicking and screaming) was the ONLY road that I was allowed to take at all not too long afterwards.

The minute I came back to my apartment from the hospital, it was if whatever bottom that was still under me at the time completely collapsed from under me. The eviction notices were more and more taped on the door; any attempts by my associate pastor to find me an alternate place to live in the area were soon met with failure; and any possible hopes for finding ANY job were for now completely out of the question.

It was when I went to services at church that next Saturday when I got what seemed to be the worst news of all. The associate pastor talked to me and told me that the ONLY option that I had left was to do the ONE thing that I DID NOT want to do under ANY circumstances--go back home to Lockney. That was to me the most devastating blow to me and my pride at the time--it meant running away from a problem that I thought I could solve. But I also saw later on that staying and fighting that problem would be an even worse disaster. When it came down to the nitty-gritty, the most unpleasant decision I was forced to make was this: to either swallow my pride and go back home to a situation that I thought was absolutely unbearable (or at least uncomfortable) OR face the music of eviction and complete homelessness on the streets of Albuquerque, NM and going through who knows what. Basically, I had no choice at all--so it was time to surrender and give up the fight and go back home.

In the final day before the associate pastor, Spokeman's Club friend, and I made my arrangements to go back home, I stayed overnight with another of my fellow church members in his apartment. I saw the things that he had in comparison to what I didn't and only then began to realize how far down I had went. And the worst part of all was this--this same young man was the last one who said goodbye to me at the same bus station that I had arrived in Albuquerque about eight months earlier (which seemed to be a lifetime ago).

The bus ride from Albuquerque back home to Plainview, TX was the LONGEST bus ride of my life. 6, 8, even 12 hours seemed to be eternity--for I was still holding on to the faintest hope of going back to the place of my personal defeat while at the same time feeling like I WAS in my spirit dragged kicking and screaming back home. When I arrived later that night in Plainview, I was welcomed home by my family, but I didn't feel that welcome back home. From that point on, my own Great Tribulation--my time in Siberian exile, if you will--immediately began in...

TOUR STOP #2--THE LAND OF DENIAL

After I got back home to Lockney, I continued my illusions of going back to the dreams that I once had and the promise that "...maybe very soon, I can still come back to Albuquerque" as the recovery from my surgery continued from my original home of West Texas. But I was in reality denying the truth--that I was so deep in debt financially that at the rate I was going, it would take SEVERAL lifetimes to even begin to pay off what I owed. Here at this place on our tour, it was at this place where I began to learn that I could never go back to New Mexico again (at least not anytime soon). The idiot who was me finally reluctantly began the process of adjustment to spiritual Siberia right here at this spot and faced the truth that for all practical purposes, the dream I once had is now officially dead.

TOUR STOP #3--THE "WHY-CAN'T-I-HAVE-MY-WAY?" HIGHWAY

Right here on this road was where all of my false pride and unrealistic hopes soon went down the tubes. The mourning period of my loss went into full swing from the minute I started driving down this highway. The first town that I pulled off at on my first trip down this highway seemed to show promise, It was actually in a career field that I wanted--but I didn't last long in it. The harder I tried to keep what I had just got, the sooner I lost it. I tried to therefore start finding ANY job that would accommodate those things that I thought were important to me, but in which I later realized were only my own whims and fancies...Can you guess where the final destination is on this highway? That's right--A DEAD END!! It's a dead end that winds up at--

TOUR STOP #4--THE HOPELESSNESS AND FRUSTRATION PRISON UNIT

Remember earlier in Unit I when we talked about "prisons of our own making"? Well, guess what, folks--this is the featured stop on our tour today. My Great Tribulation comes into the end of its first year here and continues through the biggest part of the middle of this time through this place. The inability to find suitable employment, the difficulties in maintaining relationships with my family, and separation from all that I thought to be dear all made my incarceration here very difficult.
But the hardest part of all for me personally was this: Just like Alcatraz, Lockney to me wasn't too far from Plainview--just 15 miles or so; a short 15-minute or less drive

in a car. But here in the prison that I lived in for most of my time here in Siberia, you might as well have considered it the equivalent of an ocean away. If you wanted to get technical with me, you could argue that I was a free man and that I could do ANYTHING I wanted. But I would immediately retort, "NOT in the situation I was in! As long as I was in the economic straits that I was in and as long as I was forced to live with my family, I was still in chains. I COULD NOT do anything I pleased! As far as these so-called "jailers" were concerned, I was a child and a slave to them. I virtually had no real freedom of movement. In this prison unit, I could walk all the way around town like a recreation yard in a real prison unit. But the restrictions I was under basically kept me from doing what I really wanted. I was allowed out basically for two reasons for trips out of town: job-hunting (which was very much ok) and church (which was sometimes very much a problem for them). Otherwise, I was in this prison--and that's all there is to it. That is where hopelessness immediately comes to haunt you and scream inside the walls every day or night.

But what about the frustration part of this prison unit? It was VERY easy to find here. What little jobs that I might possibly find to support myself would for the remaining   course of my residence here tended either not to last more than two months at a time or pay very much if they did last at all. Plus continuing pressures from my grandparents (ESPECIALLY my granddad), inability to get myself out of the   financial hole that I was in, and prolonged separation from my fellow church members was at times more than I could seem to bear. Sissyphus didn't have as much trouble pushing the rock up the hill as I had in getting out of this emotional prison unit.

Here also in this prison unit comes the premiere stop on our tour:

TOUR STOP #5--THE SOLITARY CONFINEMENT CHAMBER OF LONELINESS

One of the hardest parts of living on this prison unit were the times I was forced to spend in here. Sure, I had folks that I knew--but they just couldn't understand or begin to comprehend the unique situation I was facing here. Siberian winters here tend to get a little cold here not just on the outside--but on the inside, too. Not having friends nearby that I could relate to and rely upon from the times in the past when I was free simply made the situation worse. It was the rare times that I was allowed a little bit of liberty in various ways that I relished the rare chance to be amongst the people I desired to be with the most.
Here in the exact midpoint of the Great Tribulation and Siberian exile until a year later was how long my stay was in this particular room of this bleep-forsaken place.

But now, the good part of this is that we have gone to the farthest point that we possibly go as far as this tour is concerned--and that the tide of the Great Tribulation turns for the better. But before we can begin to explore that part of my history, we must get back on the bus and start heading back towards home. We will then find on this journey that our next stop on our tour is--

TOUR STOP #6--THE MUSEUM OF TRUE FRIENDS, SUPPORTERS, AND PLEASANT MEMORIES AND STORIES OF SIBERIA

But despite all that you have seen so far on this tour, don't allow the only impression that you have of this land of spiritual Siberia to be a negative one. There were also some true friends that were there for me in this difficult time here on this Siberian prison unit. Some came to visit me; others called to express their concern for my welfare; and still more arranged for really useful and practical aid for me to help make my stay here in this prison somewhat bearable despite the awful conditions that were present here. This museum was built to recognize their achievements here in the Siberian tundra and give appropriate honor where honor was due. Some are now very successful in their various occupations while others have passed on to their final reward. They themselves definitely were the ones that Jesus Christ Himself referred to in Matthew 24:34-36 when He said, " ...Come you who are blessed by my Father, take your inheritance, the kingdom prepared for you since the creation of the world. For I was hungry and you gave me something to eat, I was thirsty and you gave me something to drink, I was a stranger and you invited me in, I needed clothes and you clothed me, I was sick and you looked after me, I was in prison and you came to visit me..."

They may not have felt like they had done enough for me; but in the midst of the spiritual holocaust and Siberian exile that I was in, there were never enough of these kind and caring people. They truly showed God's compassion to me when I really needed it most. The Jewish people have a saying: "One who saves a life is like if he had saved the whole world." The museum that you are exploring now was built to honor their sacrifices on my behalf and make people aware of the memory of those who had paved the way before me.

TOUR STOP #7--THE SHOT HEARD AROUND THE WORLD

But then in the midst of the Tribulation just when you thought things couldn't get any worse--it did. On top of the frustrations of unemployment and deteriorating family relations and other pressures that I was facing at the time, I faced an even bigger spiritual threat--a church split that hit the Worldwide Church of God and that forever changed it throughout the entire world for good.

But there are some poignant stories in this episode of my history. For instance, the isolation from the rest of my church that I faced increased--and I didn't know why. For two solid months, I could not even get a ride AT ALL to church. My personal contact with the church was at times limited to audio tapes of services and occasional visits by one of my members. But in the midst of this, it was when my attitude towards my Siberian exile changed dramatically. It was only when I was finally allowed back into the action that I saw how far the damage from the church split truly was. The lady who I rode with when I was able to finally go to services again told me about the goings on in such a way that I asked her point blank, "Are you meaning to tell me that we're about to step into a war zone?" She didn't quite say it to my face, but in the way she acted and answered me, she basically said yes to that question.

When I saw the carnage of this scene for myself, the damage was so great that it was too late to repair the damage caused by the split. I had illusions in my mind of stopping everything and speaking my mind. I would have given my eyeteeth if necessary in an effort to stop the madness--but realized that I couldn't. It was in that point in time that God also had another reason for my exile here in Siberia. I found that what I once thought was the worst place to be on the earth was the VERY thing that protected me from the hidden dangers that were lurking in my own church at the time. That which I once detested was the very thing that preserved my spiritual life. Otherwise, who knows how much more I could take in addition to the current personal problems I was facing? After this event, our story of my Great Tribulation/Siberian Exile starts heading towards its climax here at:

TOUR STOP #8--THE PHONE CALL THAT WON THE WAR

Here at this spot commemorates the day I received the phone call that changed the direction of my life for good and that would mark the beginning of the end of my exile here in Siberia. An employer for a part-time job called me for an interview in Plainview. Knowing that I really didn't have much else to do at the time, I checked it out. Six months before my Great Tribulation was to end, I was officially hired for the same job that I work at now which has served as a faithful primary source of income of the past few years ever since.

TOUR STOP #9--THE HOUSE OF MIRACLES

But the Tribulation in Siberia did not end without a fight. A steady job was not enough to sustain me. There was also a CRITICAL need to get an apartment of my own (which, to me, was a DEFINITE impossibility--or, at least, it seemed that way). But God decided that it was His time to reach His hand out to me and start the process rolling for a release from my Siberian prison. It did not come easy and it DEFINITELY DID NOT come as fast as I wanted--but nevertheless, several months later and with two to four months left to go in this Tribulation/Exile, freedom from my Siberian prison would eventually come as the result of a visit I made to this particular spot. My miracle did not come instantly--but my God did allow it to come to pass eventually over time AND I WAS FINALLY FREE!!

AND FINALLY--we come to the last stop on our tour:

TOUR STOP #10--INDEPENDENCE HALL

It was here at this place where the official documents were signed that declared that my Great Tribulation and Siberian exile of just about 3 1/2 years had OFFICIALLY come to a close and that I was allowed to become independent and free ONCE AGAIN! PLEASE DO NOT EVER FORGET THIS SPOT AS LONG AS YOU LIVE!! This was the place where I first regained my independence--and I will never take it for granted as long as I live. I hope that you don't either. Take it all in, folks-- this is the air of freedom regained. Breathe it, treasure it as your own--for this independence was NOT paid through the blood of soldiers on a battlefield, but ONLY through the grace and mercy of a loving God and the atoning sacrifice of our Savior and Lord on the cross of Calvary. Even here in Siberia, every knee SHALL bow and every tongue confess that Jesus Christ/Yeshua Ha'Meshiach is THE Lord who reigns over all. It was HE who unlocked and opened the prison doors that set me free and allowed me to go back to my true home with Him. It was HIM who ended my Great Tribulation and Siberian exile and made a way where there was no way. I DID NOT do it on my own effort--ONLY HE can break the chains that bind you and me! Only HE can truly set you free from those things that once bound you here in Siberia! NEVER FORGET THAT AS LONG AS YOU LIVE!

MY FAREWELL SPEECH AT THE GOING HOME PARTY--In short, WHAT IS MY FINAL MESSAGE TO YOU FROM HERE IN SIBERIA? It is very simple--the God that I love and adore cares for you AND IT BREAKS HIS HEART TO SEE YOU IN THE CHAINS THAT YOU HAVE BEEN IN RECENTLY!!!!!!!!!!!!!!!!!!! He is DESPERATE to see you free from the bondage of the past and to take you to your Promised Land--what He requires from you is only that you let HIM do it, trust in Him, and listen to and obey His voice. For it is ONLY through Him that you can be free. FOR WHOM THE SON SETS FREE IS FREE INDEED!!!!!

I'd like to end this course with one of my favorite chapters in all of Holy Scripture. To those without hope and trapped in frustration, the prophet Isaiah wishes to give you this word of encouragement to those going through Siberian exile--the very words that come right out of Handel's famous oratorio "Messiah" that you hear every Christmas (or, as I'd rather like to hear it, during the Feast of Tabernacles):

"Comfort, comfort my people, says your God. Speak tenderly to Jerusalem and proclaim to her that her hard service has been completed, that her sin has been paid for, that she has received from the Lord's hand double for all her sins..."A voice of one calling: 'In the desert prepare the way of the Lord, make straight in the wilderness a highway for our God. Every valley shall be raised up, every mountain and hill made low; the rough ground shall become level, the rugged places a plain. And the glory of the Lord will be revealed, and all mankind together will see it, for the mouth of the Lord has spoken...

"...A voice says, 'Cry out.' And I said, 'What shall I cry?" "All men are like grass, and all their glory is like the flowers of the field. The grass withers and the flowers fall, because the breath of the Lord blows on them. Surely the people are grass, The grass withers and the flowers fall, but the word of our God stands forever."

What is my ultimate message from Siberia? Above all else, if someone ever asks you about your tour through spiritual Siberia, tell them this: "Where was God in spiritual Siberia? He was in exile Himself with me all the time I was there." If you think that there will never be an end to your Great Tribulation or Siberian exile (or whatever you are going through now may seem like to you), take the advice of someone like myself who has lived there--THERE WILL BE AN END IN SIGHT!! It may not end instantly--but in fact may possibly drag on for years. And it will not end like you would want it to--but it will eventually end up a whole lot better than you thought IF your eyes are set on Him.

I don't care what anyone says about Bible prophecy or what people say will bring the Great Tribulation upon this earth. In fact, as far as I'm concerned, no matter what other people may say, I have already been through my own Great Tribulation and exile in Siberia. One Great Tribulation in my lifetime is enough for me. And the heart of the matter is this: The message from Siberia to you today is the same one that will ring through the ages. God loves you, cares for you, wants to set you free, AND IS MORE THAN ABLE TO DO IT IF YOU WILL LET HIM!

He will turn your suffering into joy; pain and heartache into instruments of His grace and mercy; and the chains that have bound you in the past into a testimony of His miraculous power that will inspire courage, hope, and faith in generations to come. How do I know this? Because I have gone through the spiritual Siberia you've just toured through. The differences between myself and others who've went through this Siberia is this: I survived and they didn't.

In their memory, I tell this story to you so that you can pass it on to your children and their children's children. It is NOT an easy journey by any means and the price that might be required of you to pay WILL be a high one. But at the end of the road, we find this: God has given me the victory over the chains of my past and allowed me to survive the harsh exile I went through in Siberia. And the most important message from here in Siberia is this: If I have survived here even in darkest Siberia, then that means you can, too. And here in Siberia, that's all that matters anyway.

EPILOGUE: A LETTER TO SARAH

I mentioned earlier in this book how as I was writing this I had taken to utilizing the personal ads of various online services in my attempts as a single man to work towards the establishment of a more deeper, intimate long-term relationship with someone of the opposite sex. It was on the occasion of this pursuit that one woman had tried to e-mail me in "an attempt to get to know me better". I replied back to her--and then she sent me pictures on my e-mail that at first I had a problem in accessing.

But then, I finally saw her pictures--not realizing what I might see next. The pictures that she had sent me were, to say the least, too shocking to describe here in detail in a work of this nature. After a while, I wasn't for sure whether or not to respond to her at all or not. The pictures, for lack of a better term, both simultaneously disgusted me and broke my heart--for I kept wondering if this young woman had ever even known that there was a Savior that could cleanse her and heal the scars from what might be a life that has seen many hurts and scars. I even had a thought cross my mind--what if she herself may have been sexually abused or had been a victim of domestic violence? Does she truly know of a God who really loves her in spite of herself and of a Savior/Meshiach that died on a cruel Roman cross over two millennia ago that wants to embrace her as her own?

Needless to say, I've never answered back her e-mail since--and I don't know if I ever will. (She probably wasn't my type that I'm looking for anyway.) But then, it's as if He had me to write what follows anyway. Due to my past religious background, I have struggled personally to find what might be an appropriate "message of salvation". He gave me the answer to that question when He gave me the words to this letter.

So if "Sarah" just happens to be reading this book, this would have been the response to your previous e-mails--please understand why I say what I need to say here. And not only for "Sarah", but also for those of you (ESPECIALLY those that have been affected by the issues we've just discussed in great length here in this book) that have never made a formal decision to make the Lord Jesus Christ--this Y'shua Ha'Meshiach--as the Lord and Saviour of your life, please read what follows with an open mind. If you have NOT paid attention to anything else that I have said here, let the letter that you will read here be what comes to your mind above all else. This is THE most important decision you will ever make this side of eternity--the very thing that will determine whether or not you will have eternal life with Him forever or if you will be completely separated from him forever. Deut. 30: says that "...I set before you life or death. THEREFORE--CHOOSE LIFE...that you may live." I pray that above all that any "Sarah" who reads this letter will make the right choice and live for Him eternally. Baruch haba b'shem Adonai! [Blessed be he who comes in the name of the Lord!]

Sarah:

It's nice to hear from you again. There's some things that I need to say to you right now from the heart that if I do not say them right now from the get-go, then I fear that disaster awaits each of us later on down the road. You see, based on the limited contact I have had with you so far, I have the strangest feeling and discernment from my God that you might not even have absolutely any concept of what I'm talking or thinking about and that you may not have even dared to TRULY read the ad that I have put forth.

And when I took a look at the pictures you sent me, it (for lack of a better term) broke my heart because they were not to me showing me that you might be anywhere close to being possibly a woman that I might even start to desire for a more intimate friendship, much less dating or marriage. Therefore, I thought it best to take some time here to go to major pains to explain my position in a manner that might be more easily understandable to you and why it might not be best (unless I am shown otherwise by my God) to even consider meeting in person in any shape or form.

But also, at the same time, I feel the need to desperately give you a message from my God that you might need to hear that, I fear, if I do not give it to you, then you may never hear it again from anywhere else and that you might suffer greatly down the road because of it. I do not want the blood on my hands from my God from not at least making an attempt to talk to you about something that could absolutely transform and change your life. Please allow me the opportunity to do so and the open mind and receptive heart to grasp and take in what I have to say and do not reject this out of hand just because you may think that I am some sort of "religious fanatic". Instead, understand that these words may be directly from a God and a Savior who truly loves and cares for you and who earnestly desires to have a personal and intimate relationship with you.

First of all, why am I so deeply concerned about even engaging in a deeper relationship with you? It is because of several reasons:

(1.) I have a DEEPLY personal and special relationship with God and the Lord Jesus Christ that I CANNOT compromise for anything. (NO--I am NOT a priest, pastor, or anything like you may be thinking. In fact, I am VERY much single with no kids and have NEVER been married myself--but truly desire to be married if that's what my God allows. But there's one catch to this--the woman that I would hope might be my future bride MUST know this same God in the same way that I do. I'm frankly not even sure that you even have ANY relationship with God AT ALL. You may have just glanced at the ad at best and not even bothered to read the part that says that I am looking for a woman that has HIGH moral caliber and HIGH moral standards--and I honestly don't even know if you fit the part that I am REALLY thinking about. PLEASE--I beg you--DO NOT misunderstand what I say here or be offended at this--just understand instead that I am simply looking for a young woman that is interested in much more than just sex and carnal pleasures.

Why do I say what I have just said? Three things immediately come to mind:

(1.) The URL that you gave me on the pictures had the words "...sexy home pages". Finding this out automatically is a red flag to me because, to me, it does not show to me the true woman of real beauty, intelligence, and character that I am truly seeking for a wife. Plus (since I currently have no choice but to surf on public terminals), I have more problems accessing a page like this if a URL has something like the words that were on that page.
(2.) When I did take a look at those pictures, they were, unfortunately, a bit too provocative, racy, and pornographic for my taste. Please note that I am NOT talking to you about whether or not you may be a physically attractive woman. But instead, I am talking about (at least in the changes I made to the ad later on) how you may not be aware that I usually do not normally respond to anyone that I feel displays things that might be offensive to my Christian faith. Photos like you sent me does not show me that you might be a woman that shares the same spiritual values that I have.
 (3.) I especially mentioned in my ad that I am looking for a GODLY Proverbs 31: (as in the Holy Bible) woman. To me, one of the marks of this is a woman that truly shows a great sense of restraint, character, virtue, love, and modesty in all she does. Based on what you have shown me so far, I'm not for sure if you might exactly be compatible with what I am truly hoping to find in a woman that I would consider dating seriously.

Therefore, I would be uncomfortable from here on out having any further contact with you IN ANY FORM OR FASHION in regards to the terms of a romantic or sexual relationship of any kind with you. I would hope that you would understand this and appropriately respect my wishes.

But before I completely cut off all future contact with you, (in case, that is, you don't even know God or have ever received Jesus Christ as your Savior and Lord) I feel a need to explain to you the real reason for my being and living and to talk to you briefly about a Father in heaven who truly loves you and did something no one else has ever done or will ever do again just to prove that He truly loves you. In otherwords, I want to encourage you right now to decide to make Jesus the Lord of your life.

I know that for someone like you that when I might talk about God that I might be talking to you like this is a foreign language--so I'll see if I can translate what you might consider as "religious gobblydegook" into a message that you might be more easily able to relate to.

I feel that I must do this because I'm concerned that you may be trying to find the solutions to the problems you may have in your life in things like drugs, alcohol, and inappropriate relationships that have not truly satisfied you. You're searching for something in your life that you think that a relationship with a man can fill the hole in your heart, mind, and soul that is so big that only a relationship with God can truly satisfy. And you may be at a loss at what to do in your life. You might be confused, unsure, and without hope and at your wit's end on what you need to do with your life.

I feel a need to tell you that no illegal substance can save you. No premarital or extramarital relationship with a man or a woman can fill that hole in your heart. And nothing that you see in this world can ever begin to fix your problems. Nothing can fill that hole in your heart--NOTHING....except maybe the Lord God of the universe who created you and made you into a special and unique individual.

You see, Sarah--God made and designed each of us to have a intimate and personal relationship with Him. But something called sin (that is, things that God disapproves of and that breaks His heart) entered into our lives and separated us from Him--and we have suffered ever since. A good bit of the heartache that you may be facing now may be the result that you are alienated from God and do not know Him as the loving Father and Ruler of the Universe that I know Him as.

You're probably wondering, "Well, how do I get to know God? Can I do it by making myself better, living a good life, and earning that right to have a relationship with Him?" The Apostle Paul would say to you in response in verses 10-12 of the third chapter of Romans; "...There is no one righteous, not even one; there is no one who understands, no one who seeks God. All have turned away, they have together become worthless; there is no one who does good, not even one." And what makes it worse is what Paul says in verse 23: "...for all have sinned and come short of the glory of God..."

Sarah, we CANNOT be in good standing with God through our own merit or any good works because He frankly regards them as rubbish and, as the prophet Isaiah said, "For My thoughts are not your thoughts, neither are your ways my ways," declares the Lord." (Isaiah 55:8) BUT, BUT--He has provided you with a way to have a truly personal, satisfying relationship with Him.

The Apostle Paul also said this to the Romans, "So I find this law at work: When I want to do good, evil is right there with me. For in my inner being I delight in God's law; but I see another law at work in the members of my body, waging war against the law of my mind and making me a prisoner of the law of sin at work within my members. What a wretched man I am!! Who will rescue me from this body of death?" Pay attention to verse 25--"THANKS BE TO GOD--THROUGH JESUS CHRIST OUR LORD!"

How did God made this possible for you? Well, you've probably seen signs on TV or at football games that say John 3:16--but you probably have had no earthly idea what they meant by that. Well, let me tell you in a way that leaves no doubt: "For God so loved the world that he gave his one and only Son, that whoever believes in him shall not perish but have eternal life. For God did not send his Son into the world to condemn the world, but to save the world through him. Whoever believes in him is not condemned, but whoever does not believe stands condemned already because he had not believed in the name of God's one and only Son." (John 3:16-18)

There are two interesting questions that I must ask you right now--questions that you must answer that will lead you to THE MOST IMPORTANT DECISION OF YOUR LIFE!!!!!!

(1.) (To paraphrase Charles Hunter:) There are two kinds of women going through the online personal classified ads--those that are saved...and those that are about to be. WHICH ONE ARE YOU???
(2.) Do you know for certain that if you had to this very night if you died--and your next conscious moment was at the judgment seat of God--that you could go blameless before the holy, righteous God of the entire universe and have eternal life forevermore (and NOT any other counterfeit version thereof)??

If you don't know for sure, you CAN BE RIGHT NOW!! But how can you do this? The Apostle Paul also said this to the Romans: "But what does it say? "The word is near you; it is in your mouth and in your heart," that is, the word of faith

proclaiming: That if you will confess with your mouth, "Jesus is Lord," and believe in your heart that God raised him from the dead, you will be saved. For it is with your heart that
you believe and are justified, and it is with your mouth that you confess and are saved." (Rom. 10:8-10) And the Apostle John also adds, "If we confess our sins, he is faithful and just and will forgive us our sins and purify us from all unrighteousness."

IN OTHER WORDS--God is telling you that He is ready and willing to forgive you of your sins against Him, cleanse you, make you a brand new creature in Him, call you His child forevermore, fill that cavernous hole in your heart that you've been trying to fill for so long, and engage you in a very special relationship with Him that will give you all that you will ever need in this life and more. And all of this is possible for you for FREE--IF you will only ask Him to. YES--you can have salvation and eternal life RIGHT NOW!!

Do you truly want this? Then pray this prayer to Him RIGHT NOW...(don't be shy--He ESPECIALLY loves to hear a prayer from you like this...don't be bashful in doing this. Come now--DON'T WAIT!! DO THIS NOW BEFORE IT'S TOO LATE!!!! This is an URGENT matter of life and death--DON'T PUT THIS OFF ONE MINUTE LONGER!! DO IT NOW--or you will never do it at all!!):

Creator Father and Lord God Almighty, and Lord Jesus/Yeshua:

I now realize that I am a sinner and that I have been rebellious towards You and what You would have Me to do. I have completely messed up my life and am now very sorry for what I have done. Lord, I now turn from those things that I used to do that I know now are not what You want and ask that you would forgive me of my sins and wrongs that I have done against you.

Lord Jesus--come into my life RIGHT NOW and let me have this relationship with You that Coy was talking to me about and fill this empty spot in my heart that I have been striving to fill for so long. I accept your sacrifice for me at the cross of Calvary and take it as my own. Come now, Lord, and save me from my sins and let me have a personal relationship with you.

I now completely surrender to You and will strive to serve and obey You and do all that You command and say for me to do for the rest of my life. And thank you, Lord, for saving me now, making me whole, and taking all of my burdens, guilt, and shame away and for making me a brand new creature in You. I say this in the name of Your

Son who died for me, Yeshua Ha'Meshiach/the Lord Jesus Christ--AMEN!!

And now, if you decided to say the above, let me pray a special prayer over you:

Creator Father, Lord God Almighty, and Lord Jesus/Yeshua:

I give praise to You for allowing me the special privilege of helping You lead another lost soul and lamb back home to You where she belongs. And I know that the angels in heaven are having a real big time party over this right now. I ask You RIGHT NOW to impart your Holy Spirit over this precious woman and give her Your power that she will need to live an overcoming life in You from here on out.

I also ask that You would rebuke Your Adversary and hinder him from getting in the way of the holy, just, and good purposes that You would truly have for this woman. Help her find a good, solid church home in her area that will stabilize her in Your Word and get her started in her journey towards eternity with You. And remove her doubts and calm her fears that Your Adversary would put upon her and replace them with Your peace, love, blessed assurance, and hope and trust in You.

But I thank you most of all for performing the greatest miracle of all--the salvation of a lost soul. And it's in You that I give You all praise and glory for all of this...in the name of Your Son Yeshua Ha'Meshiach/the Lord Jesus Christ--AMEN!!

Now there is one and ONLY one way that I will be interested in hearing from you from here on out--and that is if you have truly repented of your sins and allowed Christ to come into your heart and life. If you REALLY meant that prayer and have done this, then I would be willing to allow you LIMITED contact with myself in regards to this matter. But it would only be as a PLATONIC friend to help you get started in your Christian walk and assist you in your discipleship--and NOTHING ELSE!

But if you DID NOT pray the prayer at all; OR if you prayed it, but did not truly mean (and only prayed it in hopes that you might impress me enough so that you can try to get a relationship in a manner that does not line up with what I have described above; OR if your purpose for contacting me in the future is done in any ulterior motive OTHER than what I have just described above; then this would be the time in which I must respectfully request that you not contact me again in any form or fashion. Thanks in advance for your understanding on this--and have fun and be blessed!

Coy RH

[Note: Men and children...in fact--ANYONE can pray what has been prayed above. And the minute you do, you will find true peace, love, joy, satisfaction, and fullness in Him. May God bless you as you do the best thing that you have ever done in your life.]

If you need some help answering some of these questions for yourself, please feel free to write or email me at one of the addresses below and I'll see about doing my part to help get you started in the right way in following Him. And if there's any resources I know of that can further help you in your own spiritual journey, I'll try to make sure that you have access to them as well. To do so, I'd be honored to hear from you at one of these following addresses:

Coy Reece Holley
@ Broken and Shattered Promises Ministries
1601 N. Date, Apt. 17E
Plainview, TX 79072
Email: CoyRH_SEATCBSPM@yahoo.com

And now, my final blessing to you in the meantime is based on Psalm 20:--that He send forth help SPEEDILY from His sanctuary in your times of distress; that in the meantime as you await His ultimate deliverance, you trust NOT in chariots or horses or in any of the things of this world...but SOLELY in those things that are of Him-- SO THAT when you are victorious, that we will all be able to as a result shout for joy. And may He continue to do so all of the days of your life's journey until it's time to wrap it up and go home...

In the name of The One who brought me through my own Siberia...

B'shem Yeshua Ha'Meshiach/the Lord Jesus Christ,

Coy Reece Holley

Made in the USA
Columbia, SC
14 April 2024

34239756R00108